Tryouts are coming up,
don't be left on the sidelines!

Learn from the pros, all the steps, twirls and jumps. Including tips from the L.A. Rams cheerleaders on beauty, diet, and fitness; the cheers and outlines from well-known coaches. Everything you need to know to give your best when it counts.

CHEERLEADER-
BATON TWIRLER:
TRY OUT
AND WIN

SUSAN ROGERSON SMITH

CHEERLEADER-BATON TWIRLER:
TRY OUT AND WIN

Drawings by Barry Cowan

TOR

A TOM DOHERTY ASSOCIATES BOOK

CHEERLEADER—BATON TWIRLER: TRY OUT AND WIN

A Tor Book

Published by Tom Doherty Associates, 8-10 West 36th St., New York City, N.Y. 10018

First printing: April 1985

ISBN: 0-812-59470-3
CAN. ED.: 0-812-59471-1

Printed in the United States of America

For D.W.M and my Mother

The author extends a tremendous Thank You to all the people who took the time to help. They were: Janice Ray—who taught me to twirl and even let me march in a parade, Betsy Woods, Loralee Wright, Sandy Thorstenson, Pioneer High School 1983–1984 pepsters, Mike Young of Yosemite High School, Jerry Alvarez, Annetta Lucero, Kay Crawford, Maggie Knipe—the twirler model, Mardy Medders and the L.A. Rams cheerleaders, Ramsey Bould, natural hygenist Harvey Diamond, Gene Casson of the National Cheerleaders Association, I.G. Edmonds—who got me into this, David W. Maury, my fabulous artist Barry Cowan and everyone else who helped me keep the spirit.

Table of Contents

Introduction
THE CHANCE IS YOURS

If you've picked up this book, you have the chance to become someone special at your school and in your community. Here is everything you will need to know before you try out for a cheerleading squad or baton twirling team.

Learn the steps, the twirls and the jumps to make it *to* and *through* your spirit sport tryout. Start now to stretch, bend and twist your body into the pretty, athletic shape of a spirit leader.

Try aerobic dancing for fitness and to develop your sense of rhythm. Listen to beauty, diet and exercise advice from the professionals—the Los Angeles Rams cheerleaders.

Practice cheer and baton routines developed especially for your tryout and illustrated with step-by-step drawings. Find out what to wear on tryout day and once you make the team. Discover the training and discipline you'll need to perform the spirit sports of cheerleading and baton twirling at state, national and international competitions.

Understand how far cheerleading has come from the days when girls stood in the stands and boys led the yells.

Find out how cheerleaders and baton twirlers today are winning college scholarships for their gymnastic, dancing and twirling ability.

Hear from the private coach of several past national twirling champions about the latest trends in baton twirling and the many opportunities open to girls like you.

Then get ready to seize the chance of your dreams. Try out and win that spot on the cheerleading or baton twirling team. You've got the chance. Come on and take it.

Chapter 1
BECOMING SOMEONE SPECIAL

Cheerleaders and baton twirlers stand out in a crowd, even without their uniforms. There's something special about these girls. Other students know who the cheerleaders and twirlers at their school are and take pride in their accomplishments at games, rallies and competitions. On or off the field, these girls are spirit leaders—models for fellow students.

More than ever before, cheerleaders and twirlers are accomplished dancers and gymnasts as well. They know how to do cartwheels and spin turns. Jazz dance, sophisticated sound systems and disco music have changed the look of cheerleading and baton routines forever. Today, girls have to work harder, practice more and start preparing earlier than ever before to win a place on a cheerleading or baton team. Cheerleading and baton twirling have evolved into demanding spirit sports that take the concentration of a dancer, the flexibility of a gymnast and a little more.

With all that competition out there, it's no wonder that cheerleaders and baton twirlers are special people. Every

1

one of them set a goal long ago and stuck with it. Hours of practicing, stretching and exercising are a part of life for these young ladies. Like the athletes on the teams they support, these spirit leaders have developed self-discipline. They are truly athletes in their own right.

Jumping up and down or twirling a baton is not the main reason students attend school. Cheerleaders and twirlers know this. To stay on the squad or keep your spot as the solo twirler for your school, you must keep your grades up. In many schools, spirit leaders go on probation if they receive less than a 'C' grade in any subject.

Conduct is important for cheerleaders and twirlers. Many spirit advisors have their girls and the parents sign a contract before they are officially on the squad. Breaking school rules on smoking, drugs and alcohol breaks the contract and is grounds for dismissal from the squad at most schools. Conduct outside school is also subject to the scrutiny of your spirit advisor and fellow squad members. One advisor interviewed said kissing at the local roller derby was "out" for her junior high cheerleaders.

"If it gets around that Mary Jane kisses at the skating rink," the advisor said, "then it gets around that *all* the Middle School cheerleaders are loose. That's not fair to the other girls."

Do you have a positive attitude? Cheerleaders and baton twirlers do. They project it in their smiles whenever they perform; they don't lose it off the field, either. When the team loses for the eighth time this season, you won't hear the cheerleaders putting the guys down.

Try going through the day noticing all the things that are going right. Now, start to climb the ladder of achievement. With a positive attitude, you'll reach the top quicker than you ever thought possible. Cheerleaders and baton twirlers are 100 percenters on the ladder of achievement. Which step of the ladder are you on as you start reaching for your goal?

Ladder of Achievement

100%	. . . . I did
90%	. . . . I will
80%	. . . . I can
70%	. . . . I think I can
60%	. . . . I might
50%	. . . . I think I might
40%	. . . . I wish I could
30%	. . . . What is it?
20%	. . . . I don't know how
10%	. . . . I can't
0%	. . . . I won't

If a cheerleader or twirler is called a snob, she might not be doing her job. As a spirit leader and someone special, your job will be to make students feel positive about your school, the teams and the spirit groups. Cheerleaders and twirlers often go out of their way to be friendly to fellow students. You can start acting like a spirit leader before you learn your first cartwheel or baton spin. Say "hello" and really mean it to someone who doesn't have a lot of friends at your school. Chances are you will put some spirit and cheer into that person's day. Think for a minute about the positive effect your new attitude will have on others. Start building your reputation as a spirit leader right now, before you put on a cheerleading or twirling uniform.

If all this seems like a lot to ask—discipline, good

grades, exemplary conduct—remember that when you become a cheerleader or twirler, there will always be someone who looks up to you. Spirit squad members of the Santa Monica College Coronettes use a poem in their guide book to remind them of their role as spirit leaders.

A Little Girl Followed Me

A careful girl I ought to be
A little girl follows me,
I do not dare to go astray
For fear she'll go the self-same way.
I cannot once escape her eyes
Whatever she sees me do, she tries.
Like me she says she's going to be
A little girl that follows me
She thinks that I am good and fine
Believes in every word of mine,
A good base in me she must see
That little girl that follows me.
I must remember as I go
Through summer's sun and winter's snow
I am building for the years to be
For the little girl who follows me.

—Author unknown

While both cheerleading and baton twirling can be considered spirit sports, there are some big differences. Let's hope your student body doesn't expect a baton twirler to lead a stomp-clap cheer at the basketball game. On the other hand, you wouldn't expect cheerleaders to come out in front of the band at halftime twirling fire batons.

Despite the differences, both cheerleaders and baton twirlers strive for an athletic and graceful appearance. Chapters 3 and 4 will guide both beginning cheerleaders and twirlers through beauty, diet and exercise routines that will help pave the way for a successful tryout.

Suppliers of spirit accessories often serve both cheerleaders and baton twirlers. In Chapter 9, we will discuss the latest in spirit wear and props for both groups. Also in Chapter 9, find out about cheerleading and baton camps and clinics.

Competition or tryout day can make a girl feel like the Monarch butterflies are migrating in her stomach. Beginning cheerleaders and twirlers will find tips on how to stay cool and calm on their big day in the last chapter of this book.

In the other chapters of the book, you will learn the basics of cheerleading and baton and ready-to-go routines for your competition or tryout. Clear illustrations will make it easier to learn the routines, movements and twirls.

As you are learning the cheers and baton routines, keep a notebook of your progress. A spiral notebook, like the one you use at school, makes a great cheerleading or twirling diary. Be sure to write the dates on each entry and mention your physical and mental progress each week. You can also use your special notebook to record your progress in diet, exercise and beauty routines. Later, when you become a cheerleader or twirler, your notebook will be a good tool to help you achieve even greater heights.

You've probably realized by now that becoming someone special is serious business. To achieve your goal, you will have to set aside time and give up some of the things you like.

In the end, though, it will be worth it. Not one of the

cheerleaders or twirlers interviewed for this book regrets a single hour of practice on her way to becoming someone special. Every cheerleader and twirler said she would recommend the spirit sports to younger girls.

Now that you've made the decision to be one of the spirit leaders at your school, you're halfway there. With your new, special attitude, learning the twirls and cheers will be exciting and fun. It won't be long now before you are at the top of the ladder of achievement saying, "I did it!"

Chapter 2
THIS IS CHEERLEADING

A sold-out game for the National Basketball Association division title between the Portland Trailblazers and the Los Angeles Lakers was just plain dull. My thoughts drifted from the court. Then, at the half, the fireworks started. Fifteen cheerleaders had the crowd's full attention.

While the music of Kool and the Gang pumped through the loudspeakers at the Los Angeles Forum, these cheerleaders began dancing, shaking, kicking and turning with the precision of a Broadway chorus line.

The girls wore conventional cheerleading skirts and tops that seemed out of place with the contemporary pacing and movements in their routine. Near the end of the performance, the girls broke with tradition completely. On the last beat of an eight count, fifteen skirts that had been held on with plastic friction tape dropped to the floor of the basketball court. Wearing black leotards with silver sequins up to their waists, the girls finished their dance. As they left the court doing cartwheels and jumps, the crowd went wild.

These girls had managed to fire up a listless crowd. They had done a terrific job of bringing the fans' attention back to the court for another two quarters of basketball. Their performance was original, exciting and very professional. But to everyone's surprise, these were not the Laker Girls, a team of professional cheerleaders. A voice on the loudspeaker announced, "Ladies and gentlemen, the Southern California cheerleading champions from Pioneer High School in Whittier."

For Sandy Thorstenson, the crowd's reaction that night was not surprising. Advisor to Pioneer's cheerleaders for four years, Sandy has seen the behind-the-scenes work that goes into performing a routine and making it look effortless. Although she is a former cheerleader, Sandy stays out of the choreographing of cheer and dance routines.

"That's really up to the girls," Sandy said. "Cheerleading has changed so much since I was involved. There's a lot more gymnastics and jazz dance. These girls work very hard to make the squad and even harder once they've made it."

Pioneer has a championship squad, but the dedication of Pioneer's cheerleaders is not unusual. Their practice and performance schedule resembles that of high school squads around the country.

Pioneer cheerleaders start practicing in the summer, devoting two hours each weekday morning and several Saturdays to making up and practicing routines for the coming school year. Once school begins, they are responsible for cheering at major sport events such as boys' football and basketball games. They also have to cover more than 15 other sports including wrestling, soccer and girls volleyball. When they fall on the same day, Sandy splits up her squad and assigns a pair of cheerleaders to go to each event or game.

At Pioneer and other high schools and junior high schools,

cheerleading is considered a sport. Girls set aside one class hour a day to meet with their advisor, plan for upcoming events like rallies or fundraisers and practice cheers. Regional, state and national competitions are playing a much bigger part in the cheerleaders' school year. While competing gives girls a chance to polish their own routines and review those of other squads, some schools aren't ready to have their cheerleaders step off the sidelines and into the limelight.

In a small town where boys' sports at the local high school was front page news, the cheerleaders had to be careful not to bruise egos when they went off to compete. For most of the year, the girls practiced for a statewide championship. They raised enough money to fund the six-hour trip. At the same time, the regional playoff for the boys' basketball team was coming up. An unforeseen conflict arose when the girls learned that the hometown basketball playoff game fell on the same day the girls were to perform their cheers three-hundred miles away.

"At that point, the boys began asking the cheerleaders why they wouldn't cheer at the big playoff game," the girls' advisor said. "The girls were very determined, though. They explained their situation and eventually overrode the negative reactions of some of the team members and townspeople."

Cheerleading has changed drastically in the last ten years and would be unrecognizable to the first cheerleader in the United States, Johnny Campbell.

In the "olden days," cheers at college and high school games were led by males only. Organized cheering at sports events is thought to have started at the University of Minnesota in 1898. It was in that year that Johnny Campbell was elected yell marshall. At football games, he led the fans in the famous cheer, "Rah-rah-rah . . . Ski-U-Mah . . . Minne-so-ta."

The tradition of all-male cheerleaders did not die easily. In high schools and colleges, boys leading cheers were often the most popular and respected at school. Standing in front of the bleachers, a squad of male cheerleaders would fire up a crowd by yelling the school spell-out. They emphasized letters and words with jumps and sharp, punchy arm movements that could be seen from the top of the stands. They used small trampolines to lift them higher in the air in a jump or back flip. In those days, the idea that a girl might be able to lead cheers was unthinkable.

Coming in through the back door, the girls first made it down on the field as pom-pom girls performing routines to the music played by the band. Eventually, the boys incorporated girls, who could be lifted in the air with ease, into human pyramids and other partner stunts. Soon the girls were leading the crowd in yells alongside the male cheerleaders. Today, girl cheerleaders outnumber males on most high school squads.

Unfortunately for the development of dance, it's a rare high school boy who can perform a halftime jazz dance to "I'm So Excited" or "State of Shock." In the colleges and universities male cheerleaders have remained. With their deep voices, they are quite effective at leading the fans in a cheer. At many college games you will still see the girls in the background doing pom-pom routines to music during the halftimes and time-outs and boys leading the cheers.

Mike Young, coach of Yosemite High School's state champion cheerleaders in California, understands the new role of girl cheerleaders who practice and perform spirit sports. When the President of the United States said in a speech on education that cheerleading could be eliminated from public school budgets, Mike responded with a letter explaining his high school's program. Read part of his letter to get an idea of what high school cheerleading today is all about:

Dear Mr. President:

I am writing in regard to comments made concerning cheerleading in your last national address. With all due respect, I feel that there is a misconception of the value of cheerleading in education . . .

This program is the only opportunity in our school for students to be involved in dance and gymnastics. Our district has acknowledged the high level of commitment, dedication and athletic discipline required of participants. Cheerleading is recognized as an official sport at Yosemite High School. Each participant earns an athletic letter. There are more Yosemite graduates on athletic scholarship at major colleges and universities from this program than from all other sports combined.

The overall grade point average of students on the Pep Squad was 3.5 last year and 3.42 this year. . . .

The greatest values however, are visible in the growth and maturation of students involved in the cheerleading program. Long after their cheerleading career has ended, they will carry with them tangible concepts of commitment, dedication, self-confidence, goal setting and the synergistic effects of working as a team. Each cheerleader realizes that the only limits to her achievements are the magnitude of her dreams and her dedication to those dreams.

But does she cheer?

If you were applying for a job called "cheerleader," you would have quite a few questions to ask your future boss.

The name "cheerleader," as you may be starting to realize, no longer describes the girl who wears a sharp sweater with the first letter of her school on the front. When a girl tells you she is a cheerleader, some clarification is needed. Do her duties include leading the crowd in cheers? Does she also perform dance routines at halftime? Is she really a song girl, or do the cheerleaders at her school do double-duty as yell leaders and song or pom-pom girls?

In most schools today, cheerleaders are just one of the groups within the school spirit unit. This unit, often called pepsters, may include song girls, yell leaders, a mascot, flag twirlers and a drill or majorette team.

Organizations such as the National Cheerleaders Association and the United States Cheerleaders Association promote the development of versatile cheerleading squads. They encourage squads to become equally comfortable leading a crowd with decisive stick movement or strutting their stuff in a jazz dance routine.

Such versatility is hard won. On very competitive high school squads, a cheerleader must be an accomplished dancer and gymnast, as well as an effervescent personality who can lead the fans in a rowdy cheer. By the time most of today's cheerleaders try out and make a high school squad, they are seasoned performers and athletes.

Jane Morris, cheerleader advisor at Chagrin Falls High School in Ohio throughout the 1970s, was a frustrated observer of the change in cheerleading style and emphasis. A former cheerleader from the "old school," Jane said she thought girls were supposed to make the crowd yell.

"Leading a cheer is 'out,' " Jane said. "When I was a cheerleader, I used a megaphone to drive the crowd. Every year, I tried to get the girls to use them. They didn't want any part of it. The girls felt they were more like entertainers. Cheerleaders are half show girls these days."

Watching some of today's top high school squads perform, you may also think leading yells is "out." But advisors around the country agreed that younger squads still have to start with basic cheerleading skills and attitudes. Learning the basics and learning how to work together are the most important steps for a young squad, advisors said.

"First, I have the girls get the basics down," one junior high advisor said. "That way everyone knows what we're talking about when we say, 'high Vs' and 'low Vs' or talk about hands in 'candlesticks' or 'daggers.'

"Next, the girls have to look as one and work toward that goal," the advisor continued. "My main thing is attitude. I want the girls to know how to be a member of a team and work together. I want my girls to enjoy each other and have a fun year. I don't want them to spend too much time getting into disputes over boyfriends."

Cheerleading on both the high school and junior high levels has become more competitive and demanding. Even elementary schools sponsor cheerleading squads. Many of the girls who make the elementary cheering squads started attending cheerleading clinics at age five!

As cheerleading has evolved into a spirit sport, the tryout process has become more sophisticated. Trying out for a cheerleading squad today is much like trying out for a high school sport such as basketball or soccer.

After as many as six weeks of cheerleading workshops led by the current cheerleaders, tryouts are held. At a typical tryout, the girls perform two routines they have learned in the workshops and one original routine. Adult judges, usually from outside the school, rate each girl on her performance. At elementary and junior high tryouts, judges look beyond a girl's ability to her potential. At a high school tryout, judges look for some very specific skills such as the splits or cartwheels.

Cheerleaders today are rarely chosen by a vote of the students. This eliminates the chance that selecting cheerleaders turns into a beauty and popularity contest. If you are willing to work hard, learn some new skills and keep your spirits high, your chances of becoming a cheerleader are excellent.

It is true. Cheerleading has become more difficult. Despite this, the number of cheerleaders has increased. One high school I know of had only eight cheerleaders ten years ago. Today, the same school has forty girls on freshman, sophomore, junior varsity and varsity squads. There are more than four-hundred thousand high school and junior high cheerleaders in the United States. Each year, many of these girls graduate and leave a spot on the squad for somebody new.

Here's how that somebody new can be *you*.

Chapter 3
IMAGINE THE POTENTIAL OF YOU

Close your eyes and imagine yourself as a cheerleader or baton twirler. How do you look? Do you see yourself with an attractive figure, shining hair, beautiful smile and clear complexion?

Now, open your eyes and look in the mirror. If you don't see the same girl you imagined, it's time to experiment with a new regime for health and beauty.

Whether you want to be a cheerleader or President, the first and most important element is you. First, *you* must have the drive that will keep you reaching for your goal no matter how discouraged you may be. Then, *you* must have a body that is in the best condition possible to perform at games and look great too.

Once you've decided to get your body in shape, there are plenty of places to turn for advice. Diet, health and beauty books are abundant on the best seller list. On the shelves of your local library, you'll find books by fashion models, actresses and a formerly-fat, Beverly Hills figure salon owner. Flipping through the pages of these books you'll find some recurring themes on how to get your body in good condition and looking great. Many of these writers advocate the same elements in a shape-up program. These are:

- Proper nutrition
- A regular beauty regime
- A good exercise program

While the path to a great look has been well documented by almost every type of superstar or athlete, there is one group that hasn't spoken out about nutrition, beauty and exercise. That's the cheerleaders themselves.

To help you on your very special path to becoming a cheerleader or baton twirler, the Los Angeles Rams cheerleaders will share their personal diet, beauty and exercise ideas with you. Of all the professionals, the Rams cheerleaders are perhaps the most conscious of a total health and beauty package. Mardy Medders, director of the Rams cheerleaders, said she often has to tell her girls to wear more makeup, since most of them strive for a natural look.

Tips from the Rams cheerleaders will also help you stay on the path to beauty once you become a cheerleader or twirler. They'll tell you about bad habits a cheerleader should avoid. They'll also have some time-saving ideas on makeup and hair care which will come in handy for active girls like you.

Close your eyes again and imagine the girl you would like to be. Now, open them and, with the help of the Rams cheerleaders, begin reading and planning for a healthier, prettier you.

Healthy Eating

That healthy glow that radiates from cheerleaders and baton twirlers you admire doesn't come from a makeup bottle. Pretty complexions, hair and figures begin with what you put in your mouth.

Obviously, to be a cheerleader or twirler, a trim, athletic figure is the ideal. From the cheerleaders I've seen, I can tell you that trim is "in" from Oklahoma to L.A. Getting your weight where you want it and keeping it there won't be a problem if you combine the mental drive to reach your goal with some common sense.

Have you ever seen a fat jackrabbit? How about an overweight mountain lion? These animals live mostly in the wild, eating the foods that nature has provided. Sodas, candy bars and chocolate chip cookies are not in their diet.

Are you starting to get the picture? Good. Now, make a list of everything you eat for a few days. How many foods that come directly from nature are included? Did you eat fresh fruit, green salads and water vegetables?

Fresh foods with high water content cleanse your system and flush out the substances which sit around and become fat. Breads and other starches, especially when they are eaten with hard-to-digest proteins, can sit around in your body for days and make it that much harder to do your best at cheerleading practice or tryouts. Of course you should eat smaller portions when you want to reduce. But try following dinner, lunch and even breakfast with healthy salads to aid your digestion.

If you watch what you eat—not just how much—you will be on your way to a dynamite figure and that "clean look" which radiates from within. Don't take my word for it, though. Listen to what the girls wearing that cheerleaders' size nine skirt have to say.

Sharyn Faeta Kelly started cheerleading in the eighth grade and continued through four years of high school. At twenty-nine, she has been a Rams cheerleader for two years and also teaches dance and cheerleading to high school students. She is 5'6", weighs 115 pounds and loves to snow ski, rollerskate and play tennis. Her tip for you is to stay away from junk food.

"I try to have other snacks in my tote bag—sunflower seeds, unsalted nuts, a box of raisins or piece of fruit," Sharyn said. "I also avoid the sodas. If the sugar and caffeine don't get you, the carbonation will. There's nothing wrong with heading for the water fountain."

Former high school and college cheerleader and a fashion model in Southern California, Babette Ray is nineteen, 5'5½" and says she weighs an even 100 pounds. Babette is an advocate of fresh foods and a cleansing diet.

"The best way to diet is to eat salads and drink eight glasses of water a day," Babette said. "You want to stay away from greasy foods. When you're eating a meal, eat small portions and don't go back for seconds. You also need to get in three meals a day to keep up your strength. When there is junk food around, I leave the kitchen and start exercising to keep my mind off of it."

A past national champion rollerskater, Donna Allen, is one of the youngest Rams cheerleaders. She is seventeen, 5'8½" and weighs 125. Her diet tip is fill up with liquids.

"Drink a lot of liquids—juices and water. Stay away from sodas," Donna said. "Liquids help keep the stomach full."

One way Rams cheerleaders Clare Maier (twenty-four, 5'6", 115 lbs.) is able to say "no" to fattening, rich meals and junk food is by "promising myself a big nutritious meal when I get home." Clare also advises to steer clear of caffeine, nicotine and to go easy on sugar and red meat. She supplements her diet with a daily multi-vitamin.

Lydia Christina Ortiz began cheerleading when she was thirteen. The two-year veteran of the Rams cheerleading squad is now twenty, measures 5'4" and weighs between 110 and 112 pounds. Her advice to girls wanting to become baton twirlers and cheerleaders is short and sweet:

"If there's only junk food, don't eat!" Lydia says.

If you think you are overweight, you will have to start counting calories. There are 3500 calories in a pound of stored fat. To lose a pound, 3500 calories of your normal diet need to go. Most nutritionists recommend a daily diet of 1200 calories for people who want to reduce.

A small, wallet-size book listing caloric content of foods you eat regularly will be a good tool for shedding extra pounds. Another counting tool should be your bathroom scale. Use it often to chart your progress.

Two big "Don'ts" are these: Don't skip meals and don't try fad diets. Skipping meals will not solve a weight problem because you will probably try to make up for the meal you skipped at the next sitting. Fad diets of the all-grapefruit, all-yogurt or all-juice variety will not help you set up healthy eating habits that will last for a lifetime. Besides their lack of staying power, these diets can deprive you of some of the nutrients your body desperately needs.

A word about fruit. This lovely food can really work for

you if you use it properly. Eat fruit alone before your main course. If you've finished a meal, wait three hours before eating fruit or drinking fruit juice. This practice allows the stored water in fruit to flush you out. If fruit is eaten with proteins or starches, the fruit combo you've digested will allow the other foods to remain in your system longer and turn to fat. A fruit and cheese dessert? No thanks.

The side effects of staying on a well-balanced diet where foods are properly combined will start to show up almost immediately. The Rams cheerleaders know that diet affects their hair and complexions as well as their waistlines.

There's no skin care product on the market that will cover up the french fries and pizza you ate last night. Baked or fried foods and sugar foods will stimulate the pancreas and cause your hormones to work overtime secreting oils to your face. Fresh foods like vegetables and fruit will help cleanse your skin from within and give your body the vitamins it craves. Don't swear off bread and starch altogether though. Remember, you are working toward a strong, trim, athletic figure, not an emaciated weak one.

About Face

A consistent skin care regime is the beauty secret of the Rams cheerleaders. Although they use a wide variety of products, each girl has put some thought into finding and sticking with a skin care program that works for her.

Cheerleaders do encounter some perils in their quest for clear complexions. The Rams girls mentioned the rigors of heavy makeup and time spent in the sun as skin damaging factors for cheerleaders. Wearing a moisturizing sunblock or screen under makeup will ward off strong sun at parades and daytime sports events. While thick make-up may be required for a special performance or competition, remember to wash it all off when you get home, and then treat your skin to a moisturizer.

Skin does receive benefits from cheerleading as well. Many of the Rams cheerleaders said that all the exercise they get allows their skin a chance to sweat away accumulated dirt and oil.

Your skin is as unique to you as your fingerprints. Following someone else's plan may be disastrous to your complexion. The secret is to experiment with products and treatments until you find a regime that works for you. Just for inspiration, here are some examples of the routines that the Rams cheerleaders do off the field:

"I wash my face with plain water daily. I use a night cream around my eyes nightly. Once a week I use a face mask."

"I wash my face in the morning and at night with a mild soap (usually Shiseido or Neutrogena) and water. I use a daytime moisturizer. After working out or exercising, I cleanse my face with a mild freshener or astringent. That way you keep dirt out of pores that have opened up when you exercised."

"My external skin care involves washing my face twice a day with cleanser, then following up with a moisturizer . . . In cheerleading, pretty skin can only be harmed by not using protective sun screen, lotions and moisturizers.''

"I wash my face with Apri and I use a buff puff. I take vitamins.''

"I do a good thorough facial once a week with an almond facial masque. Other days I just wash my face with Ivory soap.''

Spending some time once a week on a facial is a great idea. The masque recommended by one of the cheerleaders is an important step in any facial. Made from natural substances, the masque minimizes pores, stimulates and nourishes your skin.

For dry and delicate skin, try a yogurt masque, a masque of cooked oatmeal or an avocado and lemon juice masque that has been pre-mixed in the blender. An egg white with a bit of lemon juice is a good oily skin masque; or try one of the mud, clay or almond masques available at cosmetic counters and health food stores.

Leave the masque on your face for about fifteen minutes. After you wash it off with warm—never hot—water, pat on an astringent and then protect and nurture with a moisturizing cream.

While your working on your face, don't forget the rest of your body. Elbows, hands, feet and legs could be crying for some soft skin cream. Once you have a beauty regime on and under your skin, you can move on to your crowning glory.

Your Demanding Head of Hair

No matter what your hair color or type, it wants your attention. If you look in the mirror, your hair will have no trouble at all getting its message across—"Wash me. Cut me. Style me. Curl me. Condition me. Pay attention to me!"—is what your hair cries. Staying on top of your hair's demands and keeping up with your busy schedule once you become a cheerleader or baton twirler will take some effort. But, once again, the results will be worth your fastidious work.

Cheerleader advisors and baton instructors have a very definite opinion on girls' hair. Without exception, hair should be cut or restrained so that it is *off* the face. Long flowing tresses don't win points at a tryout if they fly in your face with every bounce and jump. Try experimenting with different hairstyles until you're satisfied with one that will wear well and look attractive at your tryout.

Like skin care products, shampoos and conditioners should be selected for individual needs. If you have your hair cut at the salon, discuss your hair washing regime with your stylist. Experiment with different products until you find the ones that keep your hair healthy and shining.

Living in the city presents its own set of hair problems. The Rams cheerleaders live in and near Anaheim, a freeway-close, neighbor city to Los Angeles. The car is the primary mode of transportation in Anaheim and at certain times of the year polluted air becomes the foe of clean and shiny hair.

Because of their environment, many of the Rams cheerleaders wash their hair every day. You may already know that such a regime is tough on your hair. That's why in their comments about hair care, the Rams cheerleaders name the products which they have found to be both gentle and effective. Here's what the professionals do to keep their hair beautiful:

"I wash my hair every morning. I massage my scalp as I wash. I use a finishing rinse every day and every two to three days I put a heavier condition treatment on. I use Mastey products found at the salon at Saks of Irvine, our official hair sponsor."

"Let your hair dry on its own. Too much blow drying isn't good for the hair. Letting it air dry saves time and prevents your hair from becoming damaged."

"I wash my hair every other day and give myself a hot oil treatment once a month. I use Nexxus hair products."

"You should deep condition hair weekly. After putting on conditioner, tie a plastic bag over your hair and sit under the dryer or hold the blow dryer on it. Leave conditioner on your hair for half an hour."

"I wash my hair every day. Jermack (shampoo) is really helpful and protects your hair. Regis hot oil treatment is great for your hair."

"Keeping hair clean is most important. You can save time with a haircut that's easily styled for an active lifestyle."

"I try to wash every other day instead of daily. I wash with K.M.S. protein shampoo and condition with Redken's Climatress conditioner."

While there are plenty of ready-made products on the

market, you can raid your herb garden or refrigerator to concoct your own inexpensive conditioners and rinses.

Try boiling rosemary needles to make a fragrant tea. Strain out the needles and use this herb tea as a finishing rinse. A little vinegar mixed in a quart of water is an effective rinse for oily hair.

Mix two egg yolks with a little sesame oil and you have a great protein conditioner. Apply heat and then wash and rinse. For a homemade oil treatment, comb olive oil or safflower oil through your hair, wrap it in a plastic bag and heat up your head with a dryer.

The Art of Makeup

Many of the Rams cheerleaders have been using cosmetics since their early teens. Their experience has helped them determine that in most—not all—cases, less makeup is best. During football games, the girls have a makeup artist standing by for touch ups. Because they perform in a stadium three to four times the size of a high school field, these professional cheerleaders must wear makeup that brings out their features at long distances. This type of makeup would look overdone in a smaller stadium and downright ridiculous if the girls wore it driving around downtown Anaheim.

You definitely won't want to overdo your makeup at tryouts or once you're a twirler or cheerleader for your school. On the other hand, a skillful makeup job can enhance your appearance greatly.

Makeup time-savers recommended for cheerleaders include a touch up routine. To avoid washing your face and starting over, just wet a sponge with water and blot away some of the shine. Use a cotton tipped stick to clean up the mascara which has landed under your eyes. A new application of eyeshadow, lipstick or gloss and blusher will have your makeup looking as good or better than earlier in the day. At home you can save time by having your makeup organized in a tray or series of plastic boxes near your mirror. Having a separate makeup bag with duplicates of the essentials—mascara, blush, lip gloss and a shadow—will also save time.

The consensus of the Rams cheerleaders is that waterproof makeup is best for cheerleading. Most of the girls also use foundations and other liquid products with a water rather than oil base. Babette Ray, the nineteen year old cheerleader whose second job is fashion modeling, has an outlook on makeup that is shared by her fellow cheerleaders. On the art of makeup, Babette says: "During the games we wear our makeup so that it can be seen on T.V. We also use moisturizers and powders (along with foundation) which help us look fresh throughout the games.

"In the daytime wear your makeup light and at night makeup a little more. When you're at home just sitting around, take your makeup off and relax your skin. Our skin needs rest, just like our bodies."

Pretty Cheerleaders Don't

The health, diet and beauty questionnaires filled out by the Rams cheerleaders revealed some habits the girls found to be a definite negative. The girls listed cigarette smoking and drinking alcohol as two habits which can cause early aging, a poor complexion and, in the case of the latter, an undesired weight gain.

Drinking and smoking, often associated with glamour in the movies and magazines, are more than disapproved of by cheerleader and baton advisors. In fact, in most schools a cheerleader or twirler who indulges in these activities can be summarily dismissed from the squad.

The nation's football fans may guzzle beer and smoke cigarettes when they watch the game on T.V. The girls entertaining the stadium and at-home fans know better.

"Drinking and smoking will age your skin faster than normal," says Jennifer Brimley. "They are Number One and Number Two No-Nos."

"You want to stay away from alcohol because that makes you gain a lot of weight," Babette says. "It's also not good for the body when it comes to exercising."

Give Me An E for Exercise

With all the painstaking care that goes into their appearance, the Rams cheerleaders probably spend more time in jogging shorts and sweatsuits than in cheerleading costumes. These professional cheerleaders are hooked on exercise. It helps them look great, feel great and get in condition to do their jobs better.

What's the Number One exercise for cheerleaders? Keeping your body stretched out and limber should be a priority according to the Rams cheerleaders.

"The best cheerleading exercise any girl could do is to stretch her body out an hour every day," says Babette Ray. "All cheerleaders need to be very limber. I always work on side stretches, splits and stretching out my legs whenever possible."

Once this active group of girls is stretched out—watch out! The kind of activities they enjoy range from jogging and aerobics to roller skating. Marlise Ricardos works out her legs cycling a pedicab around a popular Los Angeles dining and entertainment neighborhood. When she's finished at that job, she goes home and dances around her apartment doing aerobics for an hour.

More than five hundred girls try out to be Rams cheerleaders each year. Only forty-two make the grade. You've heard from a few of these pros and found out that they have something in common. At a very young age these girls made a commitment to looking great, eating sensibly and exercising regularly. They imagined their own potential and found the girl in the mirror was just who they wanted her to be.

Chapter 4
STARTING FROM SCRATCH

Cheerleaders do not wake up one morning and do four cartwheels, a round off, a back jump and the splits. These are movements they learn in gymnastics and dance classes. Flexibility and coordination are more important for a cheerleader than looking like Brooke Shields. It's only through good, old-fashioned exercise that those high kicks and neat jazz turns become second nature. Even Brooke Shields had to start with the basics before she made cheerleader at Dwight Englewood High School in New Jersey.

With the new emphasis on jazz dancing in cheerleading and baton twirling, you are going to need some dance classes. Parks and recreation centers are a good place to begin your dance preparation. Maybe there is an older girl in your neighborhood with a background in dance that could spend an hour a week with you and a friend. One of the best dancers I know got her start sweeping out the local dance studio for free lessons.

The flexibility and coordination you will gain from dance training is absolutely necessary for cheerleaders today. While there is nothing like the benefit you get from having a teacher right there to correct bad habits, there are dance exercises you can do at home. Turn on the radio or your favorite tape with a moderate tempo and try these exercises. After you've stretched out, you may want to try an aerobic dance routine.

Aerobic dance is a relatively new dance exercise form that has gained popularity all over the United States and in other countries as well. Cheerleader instructors often begin a day of camp with aerobics to help girls increase their strength and stamina while working on basic dance steps. Before the dance begins, though, let's get down on the floor and exercise.

Work It Out

A leotard, tights and maybe a pair of leg warmers are the ideal outfit for your warm-up. Remember that you are starting from scratch, so if sore muscles wake up with you the morning after, take heart. They're only telling you they need more exercise. Warm baths are good muscle soothers after a particularly hard work out. Also, don't be discouraged if you can't do all the exercises perfectly at first. You're going to be the winner in the end, so hang in there. Maybe it will be a month before you can get your head to your knees, but you'll get there.

31

Some dancers keep a journal of their progress. Now's a good time to start your cheerleading journal or diary. Write down how many exercises you did, your progress each day and any other accomplishments on your way to winning that cheerleader's sweater. You might also want to include special diet needs and beauty aids that are working for you.

Take from twenty minutes to half an hour to complete this series of special exercises for cheerleaders. If there is a mirror handy to check your posture and progress, use it. Please don't do the one thing that will drive dance teachers crazy and make each exercise a true pain. Don't hold your breath. You will get the maximum benefit if you use oxygen to help you stretch farther, extend higher and endure longer in the case of the stomach exercises.

As you do the exercises try to visualize your muscles becoming supple and loose. Imagine those stiff parts of your spine, neck, hips and legs relaxing and enjoying the benefit of the stretch. Not only will the cheerleading and baton twirling movements be easier to do once you are limber, but you will avoid the chance of injury, strains and sprains.

Head Rolls

Stand in place, and nod your head down; let it roll to the side, back and to the other side in a full circle. Repeat three times. Change direction and repeat three more times.

Shoulder Lifts

Stand in place and lift your shoulders up toward your ears; roll them back; press them down, forward and up to your ears again in a circular motion. Do this five times in each direction.

Reaches

Standing with feet a shoulder-length apart, grab the air high above your head with first your right and then your left hand. Stretch your fingers at the height of each reach. This will trim your waistline and loosen the vertebrae in your back. Try ten reaches on each side.

Back Drop

From a flat back, drop your head down to the floor and curl your back. Swing both arms under your legs. Count to twenty, then grab your calves and pull your head down closer to your legs. Hold for ten.

Back Stretch

Clasp your hands loosely. Lead your arms up over head and bend back from the waist. Inhale as you bend back and exhale when you return to standing position. Repeat from arched to standing position three times.

Lunge Front—Rock Back

Place palms on floor, lunge right leg forward between your arms, knee bent and foot flat on floor. Extend left leg straight in back of you. Press heel down to stretch hamstrings. Keeping palms on floor, straighten right leg and bring head and chest to your right knee. Flex right foot up. Left leg is straight back with foot flat on floor if possible. Repeat with right leg lunging forward three times. Then switch legs and repeat three times.

Leg Extensions

Lie on your back with knees bent and feet on the ground tucked in close to your bottom. Keeping the small of your back pressed to the floor, extend right leg up in the air. Flex and point your foot ten times. Clasp hands around the back of your calf. Pull right leg forward toward your chest as your head and shoulders lift slightly off the floor. Release, then pull again, five times. Repeat sequence of ten flexes and five calf pulls on left leg.

Back Bend

Do this very slowly and with a friend watching you when you first begin. The back bend will increase your arch in jumps and strengthen your stomach and lower back muscles. Lie on your back with your knees bent in the air and feet on the ground. Reach over your head and place palms flat on floor beside your ears. Your fingers should point toward your feet. Lift your hips up then slowly arch your back until the top of your head is flat on the floor. Adjust your feet and hands as needed, then straighten your arms and slowly lift head off the ground. Work up to staying in the full back bend for one minute.

Hip Releaser

Sit on the floor "Indian style" and place the soles of your feet together. Sit straight up as if a string were pulling at the top of your head. Lift your knees up and then press them down toward the ground ten times as you grasp your ankles. Next, bend slightly forward at the waist and use your elbows to press your knees into the ground. This exercise helps loosen your hip joints for high kicks and even the splits.

Back Lengthener

In the same Indian position, inhale and then exhale as your head and back drop over your feet. Return to the starting position and repeat five times.

Tummy Tightener

Lying on your back, raise both legs up and perpendicular to the floor. Press the small of your back into the floor as you slowly lower legs to a slow count of twenty. When legs are two inches from the floor you should have reached twenty. Raise legs to starting position without touching the floor and repeat the exercise. Keep breathing, and repeat five times.

Stomach Peddler

Begin on your back. Touch your right elbow to your left knee as you lift shoulders, head and left leg off floor. Repeat on the opposite side bringing left elbow to right knee. The leg not bending at the knee to touch the elbow remains extended straight and close to floor. Peddle thirty times.

Head-To-Knee Stretch

Sit up straight with legs extended out in front of you. As you take a breath, bring arms up straight over your head. Let out your air slowly as you bring arms, head and chest down to legs. Grab your calves or ankles and try to bring your chest and head all the way down. Then, flex your toes upward as you pull your head down.

The Plough

Keeping the small of your back pressed into the floor, raise your legs up. Slowly bend knees to forehead, keeping toes pointed upward. Then, extend your legs over your head until toes reach the floor behind you. Bring your arms back to meet your toes. Stretch and flex your feet to loosen hamstrings. Hold for one minute and slowly return to relaxed position lying on floor.

Wide Second Stretch

This all-purpose dance stretch prepares you for the splits. Sit up with legs open on the floor in a wide V. Raise arms above your head and inhale. Try to feel the vertebrae in your back stretching and separating. Exhale slowly as you bring your arms and chest down to the floor (or as close as you can get) in the center of the V. Hold for thirty seconds.

Next, sit up very straight with your arms raised above your head. Bend to the left from your waist bringing the right arm over your head in an arc. Left hand grabs left ankle. After a few seconds, turn and face your knee. Try to touch your nose to your knee. Relax into this stretch, breathing all the while. Return to the center, raise arms above head and repeat on right side. Keep buttocks firmly on the floor throughout these side stretches.

After stretching left and right, try spreading your legs in a wider V and bringing your head and chest down to the center of the floor once again.

The Splits

The splits is a term used in dance and gymnastics for a leg split position where both legs are turned out to the sides so a near straight line is formed with your body in the middle. In a right side splits, your right knee faces up and left knee faces out. Even if it is easier on one side, practice both right and left side splits.

To get in position, stretch into your wide second. Then, slowly raise your trunk up. Shift position slightly and come down. Use hands on the ground in front and in back of you to raise yourself up and push down into the floor.

Once you are in the splits, practice lifting your arms and hands into a nice, straight "T". Your head and shoulders are still facing front.

Aerobicise

Perhaps you have walked by the local exercise studio and seen an assorted group of people jogging in place to one of today's most popular hit songs. Chances are the people you saw hopping around, jumping and sweating were doing aerobics.

Although many types of exercise are technically aerobic, the term "aerobics" has come to mean "aerobic dance," a fitness routine done to music that increases your body's normal demand for oxygen for a prolonged period of time.

Aerobics are particularly beneficial to athletes who need to maintain high levels of fitness and stamina. Several professional football teams and many college teams start off their workouts with a twenty-minute aerobic routine.

While aerobics will not replace dance training in jazz or ballet, it can help your endurance in the field. Many instructors at cheerleading camps begin the day with an aerobic workout.

Wear loose fitting clothing or your leotards and tights

for an aerobic workout. Good shoes are important. Wear shoes that are supportive, have a well-cushioned sole, and that fit well. Also, if you need one, wear a supportive bra. If you purchase one new, you can use it for cheerleading practice and tryouts as well.

If you have at least an hour to devote to exercise, do the aerobic routines before the stretching and conditioning exercises. Doing aerobics prior to stretching makes your stretches and extensions easier since your muscles are warmed up. If you're really ambitious, do the exercises before and after aerobics.

Some upbeat recorded music, an open, flat surface and your energy are all you will need to aerobicise at home. But if there is an aerobics class at your park or recreation center, YMCA or school, you might want to consider enrolling. They say misery loves company, and when you get to the twentieth leg circle, you may agree. A class atmosphere adds to your own conditioning as well, since the presence of other aerobicisers and the enthusiasm of your teacher does rub off and make you work harder.

Baton twirlers will benefit from aerobics, too. The arm conditioners are particularly good for twirlers, because they build strength in the upper and lower arms and wrists.

As in your cheerleader exercises, breathing is vital to any aerobic routine. If breathing becomes particularly hard or forced, slow down your pace a bit. A good way to tell whether or not you are working at the right pace is if you can talk or count as you move. If you can't, you need to slow down.

Finding the right music for your workout should be easy. Here are a few suggestions.

—"Can You Feel It?"/ The Jacksons

—"Footloose"/Movie sound track
—"Jump (For My Love)"/Pointer Sisters
—"Heart of Rock & Roll"/Huey Lewis and the News
—"Turn to You"/The Go Go's

Now that you've decided on the sound, the next step is to start moving.

Go For It—A Tryout Conditioner

Jog in place—twenty-four counts.

Jog in place and swing arms front and back—twenty-four counts.

Extend arms out in a T and *lift knees*—twenty-four counts.

Do the *twist*, jumping so that both feet point to the right, then to the left. Arms remain out to sides—twenty-four counts.

Jog and bring arms in so hands tap shoulders and then arms go straight up in air. Repeat *shoulder touch*, arms up—twenty-four counts.

Side step out to right. On the second count bring your left foot in next to your right. Step out again on your right foot, and on fourth step bend your left leg behind you and *touch your foot* with right hand. Repeat to left. Continue, alternating direction every four counts. Arms remain extended out until toe touch—thirty-two counts, four times to each side.

Side kicks straight out to side alternating left and right—sixteen counts.

Jog and with arms out to sides push heel of your hand toward the two sides of the room and *circle arms*. Circle front in small circles—twenty-four counts. Circle back in small circles—twenty-four counts. Circle front in big circles—twenty-four counts. Circle back in big circles—twenty-four counts.

Side lunge right, bend at waist and touch right hand to left foot, then left hand to right foot—sixteen counts.

Side lunge left and touch toes as above—sixteen counts.

Jumping jacks—sixteen counts.

Jog and keep arms high over head, cross and uncross wrists—twenty-four counts.

High step forward three and *kick right*. High step back three and kick left—sixteen counts.

Get down on hands and knees and extend right leg out to side. *Rotate* entire leg in small circles and then large circles—forty-eight counts. Switch to left leg and repeat—forty-eight counts.

Stretch right leg in back and lift. Don't touch floor after the lift. Stop about an inch from the ground. Do twenty-four counts on each leg.

Lie on floor and *lift your* legs and hips into the air, holding trunk up with your hands. Move your legs in a bicycle—thirty-two counts.

Squat on floor with palms on ground at your sides. Straighten your legs and keep your hands on the floor; try to touch your nose to your knees. Squat then straighten again, up and down—twenty-four counts.

Straighten legs and *bounce* your head and chest to your knees—twenty-four counts.

Stand on tip toes and stretch arms up—eight counts. Walk around room and cool off—five minutes.

Now for the musical question you should ask yourself every day you stretch, exercise and aerobicise—Can you feel it? When the answer is, "Yes, and it feels GREAT!" you're no longer starting from scratch. You are on your way to being a cheerleader.

Chapter 5
JUST THE BASICS

It's three weeks before cheerleading tryouts and this notice goes up on the activities bulletin board:

"All girls wishing to try out for cheerleader must attend the cheerleading workshop starting Monday at 3:45 P.M. in the Girls Gym."

In many schools it is customary for the outgoing squad members to spend several hours working with girls who are trying out for next year's team. These after school or lunch hour workshops can be intimidating or exhilarating—depending on your preparation. If you have made the stretching and aerobics exercises in the previous chapter a part of your daily routine, you will be way ahead of most of the girls trying out.

Another way to avoid anxiety at the pre-tryout workshops is to learn the basics before you set a tennis shoe on the gymnasium floor. If you ask an experienced cheerleader, "What are the basics?" she may not be able to give you a clear answer. Cheerleaders today are athletes who have learned their sport at a young age. They may not be able to tell you how they got from Point A to center court at the basketball game halftime.

Conversations with cheerleaders and hours of watching them at games and cheerleading camps have resulted in this chapter on the basics. By basics, I mean basic arm, hand and leg movements, standard cheerleaders jumps and two gymnastics stunts—a forward roll and a cartwheel. Practicing the basics should put you at ease when tryout workshops begin.

Hands

Did you ever watch a mime perform? Maybe the mime wore gloves so that you would notice his hands. Since he could not speak, each movement of the mime's hands was exaggerated.

As a cheerleader, your hands will be just as important a tool as those of a mime. The people sitting high up in the bleachers must be able to see your hands and even figure out what cheer to yell by watching them.

At cheerleading competitions, judges take off points for sloppy hands. One way a squad can look precision perfect is to have coordinated hand movements. Here are some terms for the special ways that cheerleaders hold their hands during a cheer.

BLADES   Hands are open with fingers closed
                            tightly together and thumb flat
                            against the side of the index finger.
                            You are trying to get your hand to
                            look like the blade of a knife.

FISTS

When a cheerleader makes a fist, her thumb rests on the middle knuckle of the index and second finger. Knuckles should never wrap around your thumb when making a fist. This is bad form and could cause a broken bone if a cheerleader falls during a stunt.

CANDLESTICKS

Your hands are in fists with the folded thumb and index finger pointed up. Your fists are ready to grasp two tapers and become candlesticks.

BUCKETS

Your hands are in fists and you flex your wrist down to the floor, as if you were holding onto the handles of two buckets.

DAGGERS

Your hands are in fists with the little finger facing straight out, as if you were about to throw daggers from each fist.

Remember, when you place your hands at your hips, keep the wrists rigid. This makes for a cleaner line whether your hands are in blades or fists.

JAZZ HANDS Your fingers are spread apart and hyperextended. This is the dramatic hand movement you might see in a jazz dance routine. Cheerleaders use this hand motion for a change of pace and added emphasis.

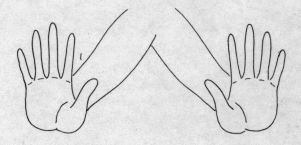

Arms

Ask a cheerleader what part of her body aches most after a game and she may tell you that it's her arms. One of the basics for cheerleaders is keeping straight arms. It is a lot harder to keep your arms up in the air with elbows locked, than it is to have droopy elbows. Straight arms take hard work. They can make all the difference at a tryout, though, so stand in front of the mirror and practice these arm movements.

HIGH V

Arms are raised up and out from your shoulder to form a V with your head in the center.

LOW V

Arms are down and out to the side in diagonals. They form an upside down V.

T

Arms are extended straight out from shoulders so that, if your head didn't show, your arms and chest would form the top of a T.

L

Form an L by raising one arm straight up in the air and extending the other arm out from the shoulder. Right Ls open to your right and Left Ls open to your left side.

GOALPOSTS

Both arms are raised straight up in the air and the top of the arms are pressed as close to your ears as possible. The football referee makes this gesture when an extra point is made by kicking the football over the goalpost.

Legs and Feet

Learning the steps can be the biggest stumbling block for new cheerleaders. The art of putting together combinations of foot and leg movements is best learned in a ballet or jazz dance class. When you are learning new steps, a good technique is to close your eyes and imagine yourself going through the movement without a mistake. A basic leg and foot movement used in many cheers is the lunge. Practice the various lunges in front of your mirror and then try adding some arm movements.

SIDE LUNGE RIGHT Right knee is bent out to the right so that it is just over your toes. Left leg is straight and extended out to the left side with foot pointed.

SIDE LUNGE LEFT Same as above but bend left knee and extend right knee.

FRONT LUNGE

One knee is forward and bent over toes. The other knee is straight and leg is is extended out behind you with toes facing front.

Remember, turn your heel out when pointing your foot. Stretch toes to point them. Don't curl them under.

Jumps

Jumps are a cheerleader's spirit signature. There is no better way to excite a crowd and finish a cheer than with a good looking jump. At your tryout, you can do a jump or series of jumps before and after your cheer. One of the Los Angeles Rams cheerleaders said, when answering the beauty questionnaire, that she thought jumps could cause wrinkles due to "extra gravity pull on your face." The other cheerleaders interviewed didn't have a problem with jumps and wrinkles. In any case, jumps are here to stay for cheerleaders, so the best thing to do is to start jumping.

APPROACH

Begin with your arms up in a V. Step forward on your right foot, swinging arms down and crossing them in front of you. Feet come together in a low hop and your arms swing back and then forward for the jump.

Do this approach before each jump. Keep your toes pointed at the height of the jump and remember to land on the balls of your feet with your knees bent. Your head, chest and eyes should look out toward the crowd.

STRADDLE

Legs are out to the sides. Arms above head in a V. Vary this by changing arm movements to goal-posts or Ls.

TOE TOUCH

Legs are all the way out to your sides in a wide second position. Arms are extended the length of your legs and hands try to touch your toes. Remember to point your toes, even if you can't reach them.

C JUMP

With your body sideways to the crowd, jump so that your knees are bent and your feet are reaching behind to touch your bottom. Head faces audience and arms are over your head, bent and straight up from elbows forming a box.

STAG

Imitating the leap of a deer, bend one knee and point the foot toward the knee of the other leg. The other leg is out to the side with toes pointed.

HERKIE

Bend one leg at the knee and wrap it behind you. The other leg goes straight out in front of you. Arm of straight leg is bent at elbow and held up in a diagonal with fist to chest. Other arm is bent with fist on waist.

PIKE

Lift your legs up and straight out in front of you. Arms and hands reach for toes. Keep head and chest lifted and facing crowd.

Your jumps can be improved greatly if someone watches them. Have some friends or relatives watch your jumps after you have practiced them. Tell them that you are striving for straight legs and arms, pointed toes and height. See if they notice your progress over a few weeks. Don't forget to breathe during a jump. You'll jump higher if you inhale as you go toward the top of your jump.

Basic Stunts

At junior high and most high school tryouts, judges are looking for gymnastic potential rather than existing ability. One way they may determine whether you have what it takes to learn the more difficult stunts is by judging some basic moves.

Practice these on soft grass, sand, a carpet or a mat. Have a friend act as your "spotter," helping you to do the move correctly and spotting your mistakes.

FORWARD ROLL

Begin with hands on floor, fingers forward. Body is in a squat with head over hands. Knees are bent and you are on the balls of your feet.

Bring head down to knees and tuck your chin in against your chest. Feet come off ground and rise above head and trunk.

Roll your body over the back of your neck onto shoulders. Knees go over your head.

As your feet touch the mat, use hands to pull calves tight and bring yourself to standing position.

Once you can do a forward roll from a squatting position,

practice it from a standing one. Forward rolls are good to use at the end of a cheer. Instead of standing up at the finish, you could also try ending seated on floor, legs crossed and right elbow on knee, chin cupped in right hand. Left hand is holding right elbow.

CARTWHEEL

Begin with feet apart and hands over your head facing to the left.

Bend at the waist and throw your body over to the left side. Catch yourself with your outstretched left hand which lands slightly away from your foot, and kick your right foot up and over your head.

Your second hand reaches the floor as your legs and feet swing around and over your head, one leg following the other like the spokes of a wheel.

First your leading leg hits the ground and then the arm closest to your body springs you up to a standing position.

Another stunt you might want to try is a one-hand cartwheel. Follow the motions above but use only the first arm that hits the floor to support you. Bend your second arm back against your chest to keep it out of the way as your legs swing upward over your head. Rotate on single hand and arm to bring legs down.

Cartwheels are a good way for cheerleaders to travel across a basketball court to get in position for the start of a routine. Have your spotter watch your cartwheels to make sure your legs are straight and your toes are pointed.

From cartwheels to candlesticks to herkies, cheerleading basics are simple once you've learned them. Now that you know some of the basics, you can go to the cheerleading workshop with a feeling of confidence. And when you're learning the cheers from the older girls, remember the most basic cheerleading movement of all. Do you know what it is? A little face movement called a—

SMILE!

Chapter 6
LET'S GO CHEER

Cheers are a bit like folksongs. Nobody has the exclusive rights to perform them. As cheers pass from one girl to another or from one squad to the next, movements change, words are rearranged and the cheers take on new and special qualities.

Now is your chance to give a cheer your own special mark of personality and spirit. Learn the words and movements of this cheer and then use your imagination. If there is a movement popular in your region, put it in. Change the words to fit your school's mascot. Once you make the squad, coming up with original cheers and modifying old ones will be a big part of your job. It's time to start letting those creative juices flow as you let go and cheer.

Pioneer Titans Tryout Cheer

First, learn the words. Slashes (/) indicate the end of a phrase:

Hey, This is the day/ Shake it up/ There's no excuse/ To the left/ To the right/ We're bustin' loose/ We'll demonstrate our strength/ 'Cause we're a knockout/ So watch out/ You're up for a fight/ The stage is set/ for us today/ We're movin' on to take control/ Success/ our final goal/ We are the Pioneer Titans/ and we are here to stay/ Now is our time/ This/ is where we shine

(BEGIN)	Up on your knees with arms at your sides and head down.
HEY	Bring right leg up to front with foot on floor, knee bent. Arms come up and bend at elbows so hands are at ears in fists.

(PAUSE)

Coming up, clasp hands in front of you. Lunge on right leg. Your weight remains here. Left leg straight to side with toes pointed.

THIS

Switch to left side lunge. Hands release and come up to chest with elbows bent. Hands get ready to snap.

IS THE

Legs switch to right side lunge as arms come down to thighs and hands snap.

DAY

Switch again to left side lunge. Arms bend and hands are level with chest again as you switch. Arms straight and hands snap as you say "day".

SHAKE IT UP

Left leg comes in from side and lifts at knee. Arms stiff and straight at sides. Push off left foot and then do a small hop landing with feet together.

THERE'S NO

With elbows bent and forearms away from your body, hands face each other in blades. Arms are almost shoulder length apart. Feet and legs are together— standing straight.

EXCUSE   Bring hands together and clap.

TO THE LEFT   Left side lunge. Right arm punch across body and hand in bucket. Left arm bent to waist with hand in fist.

TO THE RIGHT   Right side lunge. Left arm comes across chest and punches to the right with hand in bucket. Right arm bent to waist with hand in fist.

WE'RE

Lift up to toes. Both arms are up and bent at elbow so they are straight out from shoulder with hands in fists on chest.

BUSTIN' LOOSE

Front lunge with right foot back. Arms out to sides in a low V, fists in buckets.

(PAUSE)   Throw head back for a count of ½.

(PAUSE)   Return to standing position. Hands
                           hit sides for ¾.

(CLAP TWICE)   Left knee comes up and arms and
                           hands reach down to clap knee on
                           either side.

(PAUSE)

Return to standing position. Bend right arm and place right hand in blade at stomach. Left arm out to side in a low V. Both hands in blades.

WE'LL

Right arm moves out from shoulder in high V. Left arm bends up until left hand is on your heart.

DEMON—

Bending elbow of right arm circle it down to your chest as right hand palm down hits left hand which is at chest with palm down.

STRATE

Legs move to front lunge with right foot back. After hitting hands, both arms move quickly to a high V. Hands in blades.

OUR STRENGTH

Legs a shoulder length apart. Hands go to fists and arms come down to form the bottom of a box.

(PAUSE)

Arms straight down to sides. Hands slap thighs. Feet remain apart. Legs straight.

'CAUSE

Left arm out and over at the elbow. Right arm out and up from elbow. Left hand in blade resting on right elbow. Right hand in fist, back of hand faces front.

WE'RE	Left hand moves up and pauses out from right wrist.
A KNOCK-OUT	Left hand and arm move up opposite fist and open left palm slaps fist twice.
(PAUSE)	Arms are folded front, right on top of left in Indian style.
SO WATCH OUT	Side lunge left and open folded arms so your face looks through.

(PAUSE)

Return to center with feet apart. Arms back to Indian style stacked right on top of left.

YOU'RE UP FOR

Both knees face forward, your weight is back. Rock back and forth by lifting left heel off the ground as left arm bends at elbow and comes up to chest. Right arm is at side and right foot flat on ground. Now bring right heel up and right arm up as left side rocks down.

A FIGHT

Lean trunk forward like a catcher. Legs are bent. Arms out from body and bent in at the elbow. Right hand in a fist at center against left hand open towards right in a blade.

(PAUSE)

Drop down to right knee. Left knee is up and front with foot on floor. Arms bend in to chest with both hands in fists.

THE STAGE

Left leg snaps out in a diagonal. Foot pointed. Arms in a T. Hands in blades.

S SET

Swing right arm up, down and up again in full circle until your arms are in an 'L' opening to your left.

OR

Right arm moves down to parallel left arm. Hands still in blades. Face left.

US

Right arm bends at elbow and hand in blade against center chest. Legs and feet as before.

TODAY

Arms snap out to a T.

(PAUSE)

Left leg comes in and back to kneeling position. Arms at sides. Hands in blades.

WE'RE MOVING

Lift right knee up and forward with foot on floor. Arms bend in to chest with hands in fists.

Turn a quarter to your left to face the side. Right knee comes down to floor, calf and foot swing down so the top of your foot rests on the floor. Hands back to blades.

(PAUSE)

Trunk turns again to the left so your back is to the audience. Left knee comes up and foot is on floor. Hands in blades.

TO TAKE
Turn a quarter to the right. Left knee comes down to floor, calf and foot swing down to left side. Top of foot on floor. (Reverse of ON).

CONTROL
Right knee up and front, foot on floor. Arms out in T. Hands in fists.

SUCCESS
Both knees back on ground. Right hand clasps left above your head. Elbows pointed out to sides.

(PAUSE)   Keeping hands clasped, bring arms
                          down to your lap. Sit back on
                          heels.

(PAUSE)   Forward roll ending standing up
                          with arms at sides in blades.

77

OUR FINAL

Lock elbows together at your chest and place arms and palms together in front of your face.

GOAL

Swing arms down, back and up to a high V. Forearms cross at center before you bring them down. Legs in front lunge with right leg back, left leg front.

(PAUSE)	Stand straight. Feet together. Hands at sides in blades.
WE ARE	Left arm snaps straight up from shoulder next to ear. Right arm moves straight out in front. Hands are in fists.

THE PIONEER   Right arm bends in and right fist
is out from body at center of chest.
Left arm remains straight in air.
Feet and legs are straight as before.

TITANS

Right arm snaps out to side; left arm remains above head, in a right L position.

(PAUSE)

Left arm swings in half circle— down, in front of body and out to side. Arms are in a T. Hands in fists.

AND WE

Lift right leg and bend knee. Place right toe on side of left knee. Arms fold in to chest. Hands are in fists.

ARE HERE

Front lunge with right leg back. Arms punch out to front and fists are in candlestick position.

TO STAY

Right foot comes in and legs are straight and together. Right arm folds in at elbow and forms right angle with left arm. Left arm folds in and up. Right fist rests inside left elbow.

(PAUSE)

Fold left arm down on top of right—Indian style.

NOW

Arms snap out to T. Hands in blades. Step left foot forward into a front lunge with right foot back.

IS OUR

Right knee up and right foot locks against left knee. Arms come up above head and hands are clasped.

TIME

Right knee is up with left foot on floor. Bring arms down with hands still clasped. Then separate hands so fists are at center of your chest and elbows are out at shoulders.

THIS

Extend left leg straight out and point foot. Arms open and come out in candlesticks.

IS WHERE

Bring left leg in, bending knee and resting on ball of left foot. Right leg remains kneeling. Bend left arm to waist and place fist behind back. Right arm bends in at a diagonal with fist to chest.

WE SHINE

Point left leg out to side. Right arm snaps up to a high V, hands in blades. Left arm remains bent at waist.

(PAUSE)

Right arm comes down and hits side.

(FINISH)

Left arm out in high V. Face left and look up toward fingers.

Don't forget to end your cheer with a series of jumps and maybe even a cartwheel.

Chapter 7
FIRST AND TEN—
DO IT AGAIN

Combining the basics of cheerleading with the new movements will be the biggest challenge for young cheerleaders today.

The decision about what elements to include in a cheer is not an easy one. I have heard of songleaders doing pyramid mounts and cheerleading squads dancing the halftime away with pom-poms in hand. Once you have the basics down, the key to good cheerleading is to be as open as possible to performing exciting, original routines that will get your crowd cheering.

The tryout cheer you will learn next is basically a traditional ''stick'' or ''block'' style cheer. You may also be familiar with what is called ''boogie,'' ''shake'' or ''soul'' style cheerleading. The best place to learn the moves for the ''boogie'' cheers is your jazz dance class or out on the dance floor at a party. Popular dance movements are constantly changing, so be sure to keep your ''boogie'' cheers up to date. Mixing stick and boogie elements together is not uncommon. Watch your school's cheerleaders and girls at other schools to see what style of cheerleading is popular in your region. There are no rules on what movements should be included in an original cheer. Change and modify the words and moves of all cheers you learn to give them your own special touch of enthusiasm.

Containing traditional "stick" movements, gymnastic moves, such as the splits, and original movements, this tryout cheer is considered advanced for elementary and junior high girls. Spirit advisors who have seen the cheer agree it would be ideal for a tryout.

Keep your voice low for this cheer, drawing out the syllables as indicated for each movement. Betsy Woods, a young friend who helped document the movements for this cheer, used a popular facial expression called a "competition smile." She wrinkled her face in a determined smile that was defiant and almost snotty. Advisors and cheerleaders say this type of smile doesn't look fake if a girl has true spirit. Practice a competition smile in the mirror, if you like it. When you try out though, don't overdo it.

Get Up—Get Going

Here are the words with slashes indicating the end of an emphasized word, part of a word or group of words:

Get up/ Get Going/ Middle School Eagles/ are/ soaring/ up /high. To/gether/ we will/ conquer/ we won't/ hide/ our pride. Our/spir/it/ has no/ lim/it/ our / power/ next to/ none./ Packed/ with pride/ and spirit/ in/side we're the best over all/ the REST.

(BEGIN)

Full squat with head down. Knees bent, feet straight ahead. Arms straight down to the ground, palms flat on the ground.

GET

Trunk, legs, feet, arms and hands same as above. Snap head up facing crowd.

UP

Spring up to flat back, trunk parallel with the ground, head facing front. Legs snap apart to stand in a straddle position, feet slightly turned out. Arms straight to mid calf, hands grasp legs—left to left and right to right.

(PAUSE)

Raise trunk erect; head, too. Legs and feet remain in straddle. Slap thighs with arms at sides and palms open.

Trunk, head, legs and feet remain the same. Move arms to form a right L opening to your right with hands in fists. Arms and elbows are very straight.

GOING

Move only arms and hands. Left arm comes down to a T straight out from shoulder, hand in fist. Right arm moves to front, arm straight and fist toward the crowd.

MIDDLE

Move only arms and hands. Left arm comes down, bends at elbow with fist on hip. Right arm comes down and out to side in diagonal, hand in fist.

SCHOOL

Move only arms and hands. Left arm comes out and down to a low diagonal, hand remains in fist. Right arm is raised and bends at the elbow to bring fist to chest. Make a nice straight line from right to left across your shoulders.

EAGLES

Trunk and head remain the same. Move legs from straddle placing feet together, facing front. Bring both arms to low diagonals, hands in fists.

ARE

Trunk and head erect facing front. Right leg moves to front with foot pointing to ground. Left leg remains in place. Raise both arms above head in a V, palms face down in blades.

SOARING

This is the approach to a jump. Spring off left foot, swinging both arms down and cross through center. Feet then come together and arms swing back through center ready to come out as you jump.

JP Toe touch jump. Trunk and head lifted and eyes forward. Spread feet apart, knees straight, toes pointed. Arms out to sides below shoulder level. Hands touch toes or are placed flat against calf at the peak of the jump.

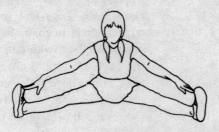

95

HIGH

Land on balls of feet, with knees flexed. Then, straighten legs to shoulder length apart. Left arm bent at elbow with fist on hip. Right arm straight out and up "statue of liberty" style, right hand in fist.

TO—

Trunk and hips pivot right, head faces front. Legs and feet twist quarter circle to right. Right arm bends at elbow with hand touching back of neck. Left arm follows trunk and legs, extending to your right, straight out from the shoulder, left palm down in blade.

GETHER (clap)

Trunk pivots left half circle, head faces front. Right leg pivots quarter circle, right foot faces front. Left leg pivots half circle, bend knee in a lunge to left. Then come up to ball of foot, toes facing left.

As you pivot swing right arm out to meet left and clap. Then bend arm at elbow and place across tummy with hand in blade. Left arm swings up and out from shoulder in a diagonal, left hand in blade.

WE WILL

Trunk and head as before. Transfer weight from right to left foot and bring right ankle to left knee. Swing right arm down, bend at elbow and place right hand under left hand in blade at left hip. Slide left arm away from left side, elbow remains bent, left hand is in blade at right hip.

CONQUER

Trunk twists more to the left, head stays facing front. Place right leg back and down, right foot faces left. Left leg in slight lunge and remains facing left. Slide left hand up to grab right elbow as you bring right arm down in straight diagonal with hand in fist.

WE WON'T

Trunk pivots front, head faces front. Pivot both legs and feet to face front, shoulder length apart. Stack right arm on top of left "Indian style" out from body at chin level, hands in fists.

HIDE

Trunk, head, legs and feet as before. Raise right arm above head with elbow still bent and hand in fist. Left arm as before.

OUR

Same as above but return right arm to stack position.

PRIDE

Trunk, head face front. Step back on right foot. Left foot remains in place. Arms in a T, hands in blades.

OUR

Approaching a jump. Cross hands, left over right with arms straight down. Step forward onto right foot.

SPIR—

Feet spring together for take off. Arms back in a low V, hands in fists.

IT

Legs and feet come up to straddle jump. Arms out above head in a V. Jazz hands, palms facing front, fingers spread apart and extended.

HAS

Finish jump standing straight up, facing front with arms bent up to chest and hands in fists with thumbs facing each other.

NO

Cross arms at wrists, left over right, fists. Step forward on right foot bending knee slightly.

LIM—

Left foot comes forward so legs are shoulder length apart. Keeping wrists crossed, hands in fists, bring arms straight up above head.

IT

Arms down to sides in diagonals, hands in fists. Trunk, head, legs and feet same as above.

(PAUSE)

Slap thighs, snap head down—chin to chest.

OUR

Slide hands up to hips bending arms at elbow. Trunk, head, legs and feet as before.

106

POWER

Raise arms with elbows bent up and out from shoulders, hands in fists, thumbs facing front. Snap head up and look straight ahead.

NEXT TO

Pivot trunk and head to left. Pivot legs and feet to left lunging into left knee. Right arm remains bent at elbow and follows pivot to left. Left arm to fist on hip.

NONE

Trunk and face turn to face front. Legs and feet pivot a quarter circle to face front. Right arm swings down diagonally across the body and out in a low diagonal. Hand in blade. Left arm remains bent and hand in fist on hip.

(PAUSE)

Slap thighs, head down. Legs remain shoulder length apart, feet front.

PACKED

Full lunge to right with right leg extended and left leg bent in forward squat. Arms straight down to floor, hands slap floor and face front. Head up towards the crowd.

WITH PRIDE

Swivel right leg front and cross under left leg bringing both legs to full squat. Straight arms, hands remain on floor.

AND SPIRIT

Slide legs out to the side in the splits with arms and hands center front down to floor as before. Toes pointed.

IN—

Splits still. Bring arms off floor and out to a T with hands in blades.

SIDE

Still the splits. Fold arms "Indian style," right over left and place head down on top of them. Bend left leg in so that heel is near your tailbone.

(PAUSE)

Hands and arms back to floor. Pop back to a squat keeping your head down. Then come up to standing with head still down and hands at sides in blades.

WE'RE

Head comes up, step back on right foot. Bring arms straight out front with hands clasped.

111

(PAUSE)

Pivot half circle to face away from crowd. Your arms swing to the right. Weight on left foot, arms same as before.

THE BEST

Feet and legs pivot front again with right foot back. As you pivot, left arm swings out to side in T, right arm bends at elbow and fist to chest.

OVER

Lift left leg until left ankle rests against right knee, right leg is standing. Bring right arm down slapping inside of left leg. Snap left arm up straight in air, hand faces right in blade.

ALL

Bring left foot down and place both legs shoulder length apart. Move right arm up and out from shoulder in a diagonal. Left arm bends at elbow and points over head in stag position. Both hands in blades.

(PAUSE)

Go up on your toes. Arms come straight up above head with palms stacked right over left.

THE REST

Lower your heels back to the floor and turn feet out, bend knees over feet. Unfold arms until they are bent at the elbow and palms are up and extended out to sides.

End your cheer with a spirited jump.

Chapter 8
ON YOUR OWN

Once you earn that very special title "cheerleader," get ready for some ACTION!

Before you know it, you will be caught up in a whirlwind of activity that may seem endless. From planning pep rallies to making cookies for the team, every minute of your day will be jammed with activity. As the year whizzes past, you'll look back to the tranquil days before your tryout and wonder where the time went.

Besides the physical activity of cheering at games, cheerleaders are expected to be spirit guardians for their school. They are the ones who send anonymous spirit notes to each player on the team when the season's losses start outnumbering the wins. And when a new dance routine is needed for a talent show or pep rally, the cheerleaders won't let you down. Then, after they've helped raise money for the school's overall athletic budget, the cheerleaders turn around and hold a car wash to pay for their own expenses. Unbeatable energy and enthusiasm are a part of the cheerleader's style in whatever she does.

One way cheerleaders are able to do so much is by

working together. Cheerleaders interviewed for this book agreed the most important element for a winning squad is unity. A high school girl, who was a cheerleader in her junior and senior year, described her experience with a "broken" and "unified" squad:

"During my junior year I was in a very big squad with a bunch of personalities that all clashed. The senior girls decided they didn't want to put forth an effort that year; so the juniors on the squad were frustrated, because the seniors led the squad. The next year, we got a new moderator and the tryouts got tougher. Everything changed. The girls chosen for the squad were the ones who really wanted to be there. We vowed to each other in the beginning that unity would be our first and foremost goal. It turned out we were one of the best squads our school ever had."

Once a squad is working together, many cheerleaders agree that good things will follow. Perhaps one of the most difficult of a cheerleader's jobs is making up new routines or cheers. This chore is easier when the girls respect each other and are willing to listen to other ideas besides their own. According to the cheerleaders, words and movements for new cheers come from three places: "Cheerleading camp, other schools and just fooling around."

"Fooling around," as the girls call it, is actually spontaneous improvisation in front of a group. A cheerleader will do a movement for the other girls on the squad. One by one, all the girls suggest and demonstrate a movement. Finally, the group sees something that "clicks," and that movement becomes part of a new cheer.

Slumber parties were a great source of new moves for one squad. With music in the background for inspiration, the entire squad would stand in a circle and watch each other dance. This method always evoked a few new steps.

It was particularly effective for these cheerleaders, since their main style was "boogie."

Popular songs have become the verbal inspiration for many new cheers, according to one high school squad. "Rap" songs, which are mostly talking, can easily be turned into cheers or chants. Even rock or disco songs can be transformed into cheers if they are recited with only a few word changes. You've probably never heard of a rock group called Steam. But chances are you've sung along to the standard high school victory cheer "Na,na,na,na—na,na,na,na—hey, hey—goodbye," actually a Steam hit in the late 1960s.

Popular ideas, trends or sayings are always inspirational for cheerleaders. The advantage of a current cheer is that the students will enjoy yelling it. Humor is another good element to include in cheers. The idea is to let the team on the court or field know the fans are there. Here are a few cheers, popular with cheerleaders that have elements of current expressions, songs and humor.

> How funky is your chicken
> How loose is your goose
> Come on all you Warriors
> And shake your caboose!

All right, all right, all right (loud)
Awesome, awesome, awesome. . . (softer)
All right, all right, all right
Awesome, awesome, awesome . . .

Go bananas, go bananas, go, go, go bananas
Lean to the left. Lean to the right.
Peel your banana and UHHHHHHH
take a bite.

Every move you make
Every yard you take
Every pass you fake
Warriors will tackle you
We'll be tackling you.

Once the cheerleading year begins, you won't have much time to enroll in Football 1A. So start to learn about the games you are cheering for, before the season begins. Reading the sports page of your local newspaper is a good start. Watching or listening to professional and collegiate games in your area will be another quick tutorial. But if you honestly don't know the difference between a jump shot and a touch down, better get to the library fast. The *Sports Illustrated* books on sports are a good introduction. A new sport cheerleaders need to know about is soccer. More and more high schools have soccer as a team sport. With the increasing American interest in what the Europeans have always known as "football," soccer may replace football as *the* high school spectator sport in the coming years. Another new trend for cheerleaders today is leading cheers at girls team sport events. Girls' sports are taken more seriously now. With the stricter laws on athletic scholarships at public universities, parents are realizing that Johnny *and* Jane can win basketball scholarships to the Big U. This has brought the interest in girls' sports to its highest point ever. Students and parents are finding girls' sports exciting and well worth cheering.

Knowing something about the sports and teams you're supporting will certainly increase your popularity. If you were a boy who had won a tough game over a rival school, an intelligent comment on one of your better plays would go over much better than the pat, "Nice game, Bob." On

119

your own during the cheerleading season, you must find a comfortable way to let the guys on the teams know you care. Think of them as friends first, many cheerleaders advise. Dates to the movies or homecoming dances will follow, if they're meant to be.

"Just be friendly to the guys," one cheerleader said. "They're only your friends. They like being cheered for, and they like to brag about their cheerleaders."

"On the court or field," another cheerleader said, "cheerleaders should be nothing but supportive of the team—win or lose. Outside of games, cheerleaders should treat the guys just as they would any other friend at school. This year, our squad chose a guy or two on the team and became his Secret Admirer. This meant bringing him cookies or a cheery note signed by his SA. Our basketball team wasn't so great, but we could always put a smile on the guys' faces with a cheery note after a hard game."

As a cheerleader, you'll be making a special contribution to a long standing high school tradition called the pep rally. The purpose of the rally is to build up the school's spirit and vocal chords before a big game. This is the place to teach the other students new cheers you want to do that night. Skits or relay games are other popular activities at pep rallies. The mascot of the rival team is usually the brunt of some good jokes. Encourage your squad to plan ahead for pep rallies and to be well organized. Like all drama, some rehearsal will help the performance when it's time for the show. One bit of advice from cheerleaders is avoid class against class cheers. The point is to yell in support of your team, not the Sophomore Class. Pep rallies are also a good place to show off the talents of all your pepsters. Cheerleaders planning rallies should be generous in giving other groups time to perform. The drill team or majorettes may be working just as hard as the cheerleaders. Let them share the spotlight, too.

Two important people you will be working with as cheerleader are your cheerleader captain and your spirit advisor. A strong cheerleader captain, who is well-liked by the entire squad, is an asset. A cheerleader captain who is bossy and yells at her squad can make your year unpleasant. There are certain responsibilities you will have that can ease the burden on the cheerleader captain and make the year go smoothly. Your captain won't have to worry about you if you follow these rules:

1. Always be on time to a game. Your captain is responsible if you are not there. Don't give her cause to worry.
2. Always be in uniform. Follow the standards set by your squad or advisor throughout the year. Don't be embarrassed by having to sit out a game because you are out of uniform.
3. Always do what you promised. When you say you will make cookies or paint a sign for the team locker room, follow through. Earn a reputation as someone who is known for action—not talk.

In most schools, spirit advisors work closely with the captain to make sure the cheerleaders keep their commitments throughout the year. Almost without exception, cheerleaders interviewed for this book thought their advisor was "the greatest." Remember that your advisor is a regular teacher at school who has taken on the extra duty of supervising the cheerleaders. In most cases, this job is fun and your advisor enjoys it. Try to be sensitive to those times when your advisor has "had enough." Volunteer to help when you can and always be cheerful when your advisor asks you for a favor. One great quality of advisors is that they are good listeners. Chances are they have been an advisor for at least two years. This experience has given them some insight to the kinds of demands placed on the cheerleaders. They have also had experience counseling individual squad members when the need arose. Cheerleaders agree that you shouldn't go running to your advisor with every problem. When personality conflicts or school problems become a burden, though, make a private appointment with your advisor. Talking things out often helps.

This is your year to shine, cheerleader. You're on your own, now. Don't forget to E-N-J-O-Y.

Chapter 9
CLOTHING, CAMPS AND CLINICS

What should I wear?

For cheerleaders and baton twirlers, the answer to this question can be crucial. A neat and attractive outfit makes a big difference in your appearance. When clothing becomes a matter for group decisions, tempers can flare and feelings are often hurt.

Luckily, there are several experienced manufacturers that can guide you and your group to just the right spirit wardrobe. As a rule, manufacturers agreed spirit groups today don't tamper with a winning look. Cheerleading and baton twirling uniforms are, for the most part, the same as they were ten years ago. Save your cut-up, off-the-shoulder sweatshirts for a novelty routine, the manufacturers said. For parade and cheerleading competition today, the password is conventional.

Skirts and sweaters are the standard outfit for cheerleaders during football and basketball season. Many squads now opt for orlon sweaters which are less expensive than wool and easier to clean. An orlon sweater can be washed by hand or in the gentle cycle of the washing machine. Wool sweaters have to be dry cleaned, and maintaining a wool sweater through a long cheerleading season can be expensive. Some schools with junior varsity squads order wool sweaters so they can be passed down from varsity to junior varsity girls. This usually happens when the school is footing the cheerleaders' wardrobe bill. In most cases, however, cheerleaders pay for their own outfits and accessories.

One unique part of your sweater is the emblem. With your squad, you will chose a block letter or mascot emblem. The manufacturer will stitch your name on the letter or symbol. Emblems come in wool or orlon chenille and can be taken off your sweater at the end of the season. The emblem makes a nice keepsake, when you are required to pass your sweater on to a younger girl.

A cheerleader's wardrobe consists of a winter uniform, spring uniform and summer uniform. Winter uniforms, usually skirts and sweaters, are the heaviest and used for outdoor events. In very cold regions, some squads purchase matching capes or snow suits to wrap up in between cheers. Spring uniforms can be jumpers and blouses or light-weight skirts and sweaters. Cheerleaders also wear the spring uniforms for indoor events such as basketball and wrestling. Cotton jumpers, or cotton skirts and tops, are the traditional summer uniforms worn at cheerleading camps and clinics. Many squads wear these cooler uniforms to school on game days, too.

If you are selected to cheer for the entire school year, plan on spending at least $500 for your wardrobe. Several manufacturers said some high school and college squads spent as much as $800 per cheerleader on clothing and accessories.

Once you make the squad, your spirit advisor may have some ideas about how you can earn money to pay for your uniforms. Listen, too, to your advisor's suggestions on selecting outfits that look flattering on all the cheerleaders in your group. Your advisor knows the score when he or she gives you the following advice:

1. Hips and tummys look better when the pleats are sewn down from the waist to the top of the legs.
2. Avoid sweaters that are too large. When ordering sweaters with stripes around the waistband, make sure the stripes will show.
3. Order an extra pair of pom-poms, socks and tights. Ordering all your items at the same time, instead of later in the season, will ensure they are from the same dye lot.
4. Keep skirt lengths consistent. Shorter skirts accent heavy and skinny thighs.
5. Choose comfortable, supportive footwear. Shoes designed for aerobic dance class are ideal. They will support your weight when you jump.

The secret of a sharp-looking squad is uniformity. If you plan to wear ribbons in your hair, try to buy a few extra yards so everyone on the squad will have the same hair ornaments. Most squads don't allow members to wear lots of jewelry. A watch, class ring and your cheerleader megaphone necklace may be the only pieces you will wear when you are in uniform.

One occasion when you will want to leave your uniform home in the closet is when the squad is planning a novelty routine. Novelty routines are special dance routines or cheers performed only once and following a set theme. Props for novelty routines can include beach balls, hats and canes, balloons, masks and anything else that will add some excitement to a routine. Squads save their hottest movements and stunts for novelty routines. Here's where elements from new forms of dance such as "breaking" and "popping" will appear.

If your squad uses pom-poms, make sure to keep them dry. Paper pom-poms especially should always be transported in plastic bags. Many squads today use metallic or plastic pom-poms. They are waterproof, look attractive from a distance and don't shed their color on your hands and uniform. An average pom-pom is made with 3,000 to 5,000 strands. It's important to keep these strands off the basketball court after a routine. Most squads leave time for a quick clean-up after basketball halftime.

In addition to pom-poms, your cheerleading supplier may also offer school spirit boosters. Pins, ribbons, cups, hats and oversized foam hands that proclaim your team as #1 are some of the many school spirit accessories available. Cheerleaders can order these items in bulk and then sell them to students before the games. Most companies will allow your squad to send an original design. In a rush, the cheerleader suppliers will also take telephone orders.

The busiest months for manufacturers of cheerleading uniforms are April through December. Some manufacturers offer discounts for items ordered during the slow period, before the new cheerleading squads are selected. Another way to save money on uniforms is to sew them at home. Cheerleader Supply Co. of Dallas, Texas offers pre-cut skirts at half the ready-made price.

You may want to write for a cheerleader supply catalog. The majority of the supply companies are located in Texas, the state that seems to have more cheerleaders than cowboys! Write for uniform and supply information to:

> Cheerleader Supply Co.
> P.O. Box 30674
> Dallas, TX 75230
>
> Spirit Leaders
> P.O. Box 31547
> Dallas, TX 75231

There's nothing wrong with dreaming about how great you will look in your cheerleading uniform, but don't forget, tryouts come first. You will be required to wear your gym uniform or a standard pair of shorts and T-shirt for the tryout. Be sure that your outfit is freshly pressed and that your sport shoes are clean or polished. Wear ribbons or barrettes that are in the school colors, but don't overdo by wearing every spirit pin you've collected in the last year. Keep your makeup to a minimum for a fresh look. Remember, also, the one most important rule of all: Keep your hair off your face. Let the judges see the spirit in your eyes, not your bangs.

The standard uniform for baton twirlers is a skin-tight body suit with a zipper in the back and shoulder straps. Resembling a sleeveless leotard or a bathing suit, the baton twirler uniforms are made from heavier material, usually a shiny, stretch nylon. Decorations on a twirler's uniform may consist of appliques, beading, sequins or fringe.

Footwear for twirlers is usually an athletic or jazz dance shoe that gives good support to the feet and arches. Marching baton twirlers need comfortable shoes for the long parade routes. Boots, which were popular with marching groups in the past, are considered out of style.

Marching baton twirlers or majorettes may discard the

standard, leotard-type uniform in favor of special costumes which represent the school's name or mascot. The Middle School Patriots might be a majorette team whose members wear costumes depicting the Revolutionary War era. Some baton twirling groups have more than one outfit for performances. The Central High Indians might have Indian costumes for parades and standard twirling suits for athletic events.

A popular extra for baton twirlers are warm-up suits or jackets. Competitive twirlers wear the warm up gear before and after their routines. Marching twirlers often have jackets to wear after a parade or with their street clothes at school.

Choosing a Camp

Summertime is practice time for baton twirlers and cheerleaders. It's also time for attending baton or cheerleading camps.

There are several baton and cheerleading camps held each summer, right in your area. Stop by your physical education teacher's classroom and ask her to let you look at some brochures on spirit camps. Your local park and recreation director might have a stack of literature on camps in your area, too. One new trend in cheerleading camps is camps run for younger girls by a high school squad. By teaching basics and some easy cheers to elementary and junior high girls, the cheerleaders earn money for their upcoming year.

Held on college campuses or in summer resort areas, cheerleading camps have become a summer tradition. Cheerleaders spend from Sunday to Thursday nights in the college dorms or other sleeping areas. Days are spent outside learning new skills and routines. At camp, cheerleaders have a unique chance to meet girls from other schools, outside the tense atmosphere of a game or competition. Instructors at the camps are usually college cheerleaders who have several years experience teaching cheers and performing them.

At most cheerleading camps, part of the day is spent watching other squads perform. Instructors judge each squad on technique, execution and spirit. Comments from other squads also help cheerleaders improve their style before the fall and winter sports seasons begin.

Girls who have not yet been selected for a cheerleading squad may attend camp if they wish. Most overnight camps, though, are geared for squads. The exception would be the camps run by the high school cheerleaders. If you want to go to cheerleading camp alone or with a friend, you may want to chose a program that doesn't center around squads.

A week-long cheerleading camp session may cost up to $150. A cheaper way to go is clinics. Many of the same companies that run the summer cheerleading camps also sponsor weekend clinics at the park or schools. Girls not yet part of a squad will probably find the clinics better suited to their needs.

Don't forget your cheerleading notebook when you go to camp. Once you're home, it's difficult to remember that snappy chant or the moves to a cheer. You'll want to write down the addresses of girls you meet from other cities and states, too.

Baton camps are geared more toward solo twirlers. If you

are a member of a majorette team, you may want to attend a drill team camp. These camps stress group performance and choreography which helps teams improve their overall look.

Solo twirlers headed for a season of tough competition may want to save their money for baton lessons, instead of camp. Individual attention from your coach or teacher might be more worthwhile to solo twirlers than the group work at a camp. Perhaps the best candidates for baton camp are beginning twirlers who are just learning their spins, how to march and how to put a routine together for competition.

When you and your parents are deciding on a cheerleading or baton camp, ask older girls about their experiences at various camps. Were the instructors helpful and encouraging? How many girls were in the average teaching sessions? Did they learn something really new each day? Find out the answers to these questions before you make a decision about camp.

For news about cheerleading, baton and drill team camps around the United States, a good source is *Let's Cheer* magazine. Baton and cheerleading camps are advertised in this national publication each spring. Write, *Let's Cheer*, 1212 Ynez, Redondo Beach, CA 90277.

For news and advertisements concerned strictly with baton twirling, try the following publications: Drum Major Magazine, P.O. Box 266, Janesville, Wisconsin 53545. (Drum Major is the official publication of the National Baton Twirling Association, NBTA.) Twirl Magazine, 340 Maynard Building, 119 First Avenue South, Seattle, Washington 98104. (Twirl is the official publication of the United States Twirling Association, USTA.)

When you're packing for camp, don't forget to bring the most important part of your cheerleading or twirling wardrobe. That's right . . . your smile!

Chapter 10
THIS IS TWIRLING

Start talking about baton twirling and a funny thing happens. People whom you never suspected had any interest in parades, marching bands or school spirit, start bringing out their old majorette jackets, batons and yearbooks.

Many adults interviewed for this book remember their majorette days as some of the happiest in their lives. A popular bumper sticker often seen on cars at parades and competitions reads, "Twirlers have more fun."

When you pick up a baton and learn your first twirl, you'll quickly find out why there are more than one million baton twirlers in the United States alone. Making that shiny piece of metal spin like the dickens *is* fun. Tossing a baton up in the air and catching it is *really* fun. Even dropping the baton makes you laugh at yourself and try a little harder the next time.

If you do some detective work around your city or town, you will probably discover that there is a twirling group you can join right away. While there are usually tryouts for high school twirling teams, many junior high and elementary-level teams have coaches that will teach you the routines and how to twirl, too.

Studying baton with an experienced teacher is really the best way to go for this sport. Another funny thing about baton twirling is that finding a teacher will be easier than you think.

Two young girls I know decided to change their image when they entered high school. They wanted to be a part of things for once instead of just sitting on the sidelines and—literally—watching the parade go by.

To prepare for their new lives, the girls spent the summer before ninth grade practicing baton twirling on the wide lawn in front of one of their homes. By the end of the summer, the girls had had a lot of fun, but they were still rookie twirlers.

Then a few weeks before twirling team tryouts a funny thing happened. While the two girls were practicing baton on the lawn, a college girl drove past, stopped, backed up and got out of her car.

"No, no, no. You're doing it all wrong," the older girl said. "It goes like this."

For the next two weeks, the college girl took the time to show basic baton techniques to her willing pupils. The girls soon discovered that their volunteer teacher was a former state champion twirler.

By the time majorette tryouts were held, the girls were ready. Thanks to their own decision to get involved and the thoughtful help of an unsolicited teacher, the girls made it. For the next four years they represented their high school as majorettes.

Once they made the team, the girls found out, as you will, that the benefits of baton twirling go beyond the glory of performing at parades and halftime shows.

One thing you won't be doing at parades is standing still. All that marching requires physical fitness. The practice you will do to look precision perfect at the parade will get you in shape. If you follow the exercise, diet and beauty suggestions in Chapters 3 and 4, along with your regular parades and practice routines, people will start noticing your movements even when you are out of uniform. You will look and feel great and start walking the halls at school with a new confidence.

As you improve your twirling, you will become aware of all the different parts of your body and how they can work together as a unit. Studying your routines in front of a mirror, you will strive to make each movement more graceful. Just as you can pick out a girl who looks like a ballet dancer, you can pick out an accomplished twirler. She holds her head and neck high and seems to have a bouncy spring in her walk. Accomplished twirlers carry themselves with a style and grace that becomes high fashion models. Gracefulness is another benefit you will gain when you learn to twirl.

There is a very independent and individual part of twirling. It's called practice. You will soon learn that no one else can do this for you. As you develop good practice habits, you will be setting a pattern for discipline that you can carry into your future school and working life. If you are part of a twirling group, you will have the added benefit of learning teamwork. Practice on your own will be even more important, since it will later add to the group effort.

There's something else that is wonderful about baton twirling. No matter how hard you practice, sweat and practice some more—it pays off. The opportunities available to baton twirlers seem to multiply each year.

Two hundred colleges and universities in the United

States offer scholarships to solo twirlers selected to lead their bands. Some of the schools where you can twirl for your tuition include: University of Kansas at Laurence; Purdue University; University of Michigan; Texas Christian University in Fort Worth; Penn State University; College of William and Mary in Virginia; Memphis State University and the University of Hawaii.

Competition opportunities for baton twirlers are snowballing. The first World Baton Twirling Championships were held in Seattle in 1980. Since then, more than five million twirlers—both boys and girls—have competed in the same event in Tokyo, France, Italy, and Canada. There are state, regional and national competitions as well—more than five hundred contests annually in the U.S. There were seven thousand twirlers competing at the National Open Championships sponsored by the United States Twirling Association in 1983.

One of the best benefits of twirling is friendships. In parades and at competitions you will meet girls and boys from other schools, towns, states and even other countries. Baton twirlers have practiced smiling for years and somehow those smiles stay on when they meet new people. One of the first baton movements you may want to learn is the salute. This is the traditional way majorettes say "Howdy!" when they see each other in marching costume.

You will contribute to your community as a baton twirler. I once lived in a small town called Tracy, California that had thirteen parades a year. There were homecoming parades, Christmas parades, Fourth of July parades, Veteran's Day parades and religious parades.

As a reporter for the community newspaper, I often wondered how I could ever get a fresh angle on another parade story. Yet each time I took my camera and notebook out to Main Street on parade day, I ended up coming back with a roll of pictures and a notebook full of quotes.

The people watching the parade were always a great story. Grandpas on their porch steps and young children on their fathers' shoulders strained to watch the last twirler go by. The joy on their faces seemed to make each of the thirteen parades worthwhile.

Once you've decided that twirling is for you, you're going to need support from your family. Majorette uniforms cost money. You might also want to attend baton twirling camps or clinics. They cost money, too. When you have a parade in another town, you'll have to arrange transportation.

Sit down with your family and discuss the finances and logistics of baton twirling. Make sure they understand you are committed to taking up this sport seriously. Ask your family members to help you find ways to earn money for uniforms or camp. Once they become a part of your effort, you'll be surprised at how your twirling career will take off. It will be awfully hard to watch TV when your little brother asks you if you've done your baton practice yet.

How it all started

The sport of baton twirling has come such a long way from its early beginnings, that many of today's twirlers never march in a parade. They are solo twirlers who look forward to performing their original routines in competition.

Despite the widening gap between majorettes or marching twirlers and competition twirlers, members of both groups had to start out learning the basics—from how to march to which end of the baton is which!

One of the earliest written records of a drum major leading a marching unit comes from the High Renaissance period in England. Brandishing a two-handed broadsword, the "Master Drummer" cleared the way for marching soldiers during the reign of King Edward VI (1547–1553).

By the 1600s, "Drummer Majors," as they were then called, acquired another, more warlike duty. They were required to carry a "cat o' nine tails," a baton with strips of metal-tipped leather, and administer lashes to disobedient soldiers.

The next development in twirling came in the early 1700s when the "Twirling Drum Major" led the British Army's Jainzery Band. Carrying a pole with attached metal crescents and suspended bells, this early twirler regulated the marching and music. The British Army patterned their colorful band after the marching troops they had seen on campaigns in Turkey. The pole, known in Turkey as a crescent pole, was called a Jingling Johnny in England.

In 1844, Queen Victoria abolished the Jainzery or Turkish bands. The drum major remained in the more conventional bands, however, carrying a pole without sticks or bells. He continued to lead the band and practice the movements, tosses and tricks of the Jingling Johnny days.

In Eastern cultures, twirling began with ceremonial dances performed with spears, lances or knives. Skilled performers in Siam manipulated lances with bells on either end in rolls across their shoulders, arms and backs.

Twirling also has a history in the ancient cultures of island people. During special celebrations, Samoan dancers spin cane knives with long bamboo handles and sharp blades.

A New World beginning for twirling can be traced to the wine carriers who accompanied marching bands in the United States during the 1800s. Holding long poles with round jugs attached at the top, carriers transported wine for the marchers. While they marched, the wine carriers entertained the crowd with twirls and balancing movements of the pole. Eventually, the jug was abandoned and carriers used smaller poles to do the intricate spins and twirls without risking spilling the wine.

It was Americans who eventually popularized the sport of baton twirling. Kay Crawford, founder of the Miss Drill Team U.S.A. pageant and a baton teacher for more than thirty years, traces the origins of the sport to World War I. In military parades at home and abroad, American soldiers twirled their rifles while marching. Lighter wooden guns were eventually substituted for the real thing. Finally, a trim metal baton, with steel ball and tip was used. Old time batons were much longer and heavier than the ones used today, Kay said.

Not far behind the Americans were the Japanese, who recognized the benefits of twirling on coordination and concentration. Baton twirling is taught as a required course in many of the elementary schools in Japan. In 1983, for the first time ever, three Japanese twirlers broke the U.S. monopoly on world twirling titles. At the world championships in Milan, Italy, two Japanese twirlers placed second and third in the men's competition. A young Japanese girl took third place in the junior women's competition. This marked the first time U.S. baton twirlers failed to sweep all the first, second and third place trophies at the world competition.

Your baton

BALL   SHAFT   TIP

Today's batons are descendants of the swords, poles, lances and spears of drum majors and ceremonial dancers. A modern baton is made of lightweight metal. It has rubber coverings or "mushrooms" at each end. The larger and heavier covering is called the ball. The smaller covering is called the tip. The baton metal between these two ends is the shaft.

A standard baton costs about nine dollars. Batons can usually be purchased at sport or music stores or from your baton teacher. Your baton should be the same length as the distance from underneath your arm to the end of your middle finger. If you are unable to locate a baton supplier in your area, here are a few companies that will send you a catalogue:

> Sharp's Baton Mfg. Co.
> 1122 S. Main Street
> Elkhart, Indiana 46516

> Star Line Baton Co.
> P.O. Box 5490
> Pompano Beach, Florida 33064

> Cathy's Twirling Accessories
> 1372 Camino Robles Way
> San Jose, CA 95120

ABC-American Baton Co.
300 S. Wright Rd.
Janesville, Wisconsin 53545

Taking care of your shiny, new baton will be quite simple. Use a soft cloth to wipe the metal shaft after each use. This will preserve the chrome finish. Rubber ends can be cleaned with household cleaners or white shoe polish on parade days. Majorettes often cover the ends of a newly-polished baton with plastic bags until just before the parade begins.

Drill

Before you learn to twirl, you must know how to hold the baton correctly and how to march. There are ten standard commands used for marching with a baton. Practice each of these movements thoroughly. Ask a friend to test you by calling out commands in a random order.

Attention

Hands are on hips below your waist. Baton is in your right hand with fingers front and thumb hidden. Now bring both arms above your head so ball points upward.

Return arms to waist and baton to cradle of arm, ball down.

At ease

From final attention position, move left foot to shoulder width from right foot.

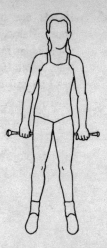

Swing baton down behind back
and grasp shaft near the ends.
Only move your left foot when you
resume attention from at ease
position.

Mark time

Begin in final attention position. Bring left foot and knee up and raise right arm and ball of baton up. Baton comes down to your right hip bone as your left foot hits the floor and right knee comes up. Practice in place, lifting knees equal height each time. Feet touch the ground with the balls first, not heels. Marking time is marching in place.

March forward

Move forward as you march. Keep head and shoulders erect and point toes down as you bring your knees up. Your drill leader will tell you whether or not you should let your left arm go free and follow the march, swinging opposite of the right. When in a group, make sure your steps are equal to the other girls. Stay in your line or rank as you move along the parade route.

Halt	Take three steps after the drill leader blows her whistle or calls out the command, Halt! Since you always begin marching on the left foot—step left, right, and come to a stop as your left foot comes firmly to the ground.
Right face	Bend left knee slightly and pivot on ball of right foot. Turn your body one quarter circle to the right. Begin from and resume attention position when you move right face.
Left face	Same as above, but reverse it. Bend right knee and pivot on left foot a quarter circle.
About face	Place your right toe behind your left heel. Left toes are arched up slightly. Pivot with feet in this position a half circle so you are facing the opposite direction. Practice having your feet finish in attention position without adjusting them.
Dress right	As a horizontal line of girls moves down the street, all of them, with the exception of the girl at the far right, look to the right to make

	sure the line is straight. The girl at the end of the line or rank looks left and makes sure she is in line, too.
To the rear	As you are marching forward, step left and then pivot on that foot a half circle to the right and then step right. This has the same effect of turning you around as about face, without the more pronounced pivot.

The Salute

At parades and competitions, twirlers have a special way of saying "hello." It's called the salute.

You will want to learn this movement and practice it often. Salutes should be sharp and done with precision. A snappy salute is often the first impression people will have of you as a twirler.

Salutes are also used when a twirling group or solo twirler and band pass the judges' reviewing stand at a parade. Many parade routines have a form of a salute in the very beginning to say "hello" to the crowd. When the American flag passes, a salute is the proper response.

1. Begin your salute in the attention position with your baton cradled on right arm.

2. Bring baton with tip leading straight out in front of you. Circle baton down to your feet and up behind your back.
3. Open your palm and hold the shaft between the thumb and first finger. Now, bring the baton to your shoulder, so it hangs down vertically. The back of your right hand rests against the left shoulder and the baton has the ball up and tip down.

Chapter 11
BATON BASICS

Here's a story about a young girl who wasn't afraid to try.

At age 5, Annetta asked her mother, a baton teacher, to let her begin taking lessons. Her mother said "No." Finally, after Annetta pestered her for several weeks, the mother told her young daughter she could begin lessons only if she learned to do four elbow rolls—a difficult trick—and a neck roll—a more difficult trick—in two weeks. Fourteen days later, Annetta showed her mother the required tricks and her twirling career began.

At age 16, Annetta Lucero won the biggest honor in twirling—the Senior Women's World Champion title. Looking back, she realizes why her mother had been against teaching her to twirl.

"She didn't want me to spend my whole life practicing," Annetta said. "I know now what baton twirling is. It's a competitive, hard-working sport."

Perhaps the most important point in any twirler's career is the starting point. The time to develop good baton techniques is right now. If you are serious about learning to twirl, set aside a scheduled time each day for practice. The year before Annetta won the world title, she was practicing more than five hours a day. When her tryout time came at the world championships, Annetta wasn't afraid to try. She was ready.

In any organized sport there are standards. In basketball, standards dictate how high the hoop should be set. In tennis, standards set the height of the net, length of the court and match rules. The organization that sets standards for twirlers in this country is the United States Twirling Association (USTA).

The USTA was formed in 1958 to promote baton twirling in the United States and abroad. The association gives teachers, students, parents and contest judges information about baton twirling standards. You may want to write the USTA for an information booklet or a subscription to the baton magazine *Twirl*. Write USTA, 340 Maynard Building, 119 First Avenue South, Seattle, WA 98104.

Although there are many variations on the names of baton tricks, and twirls, those described here follow USTA standards. Your mom, sister or neighbor may tell you another name for the tricks, but if you learn the *standard* name as set by the USTA, you will be ahead of the game at baton camps, clinics and competitions.

WRIST TWIRL

Hold your baton at the center of the shaft. Turn your wrist loosely until the ball circles close to your side or on the inside. The tip of the baton is always on the outside in a wrist twirl. Practice doing several circles holding the baton in each hand.

FIGURE 8

With your elbow bent slightly, hold the baton in the center, thumb toward the ball, and then move it down to the right side and then the left.

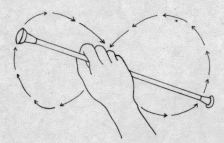

Imagine you are drawing a sideways 8 or scooping ice cream from a barrel of vanilla on the right side and chocolate on the left. Your hand turns over in this twirl. Practice with both right and left hands.

REVERSE FIGURE 8 Hold baton in your right hand with the ball up and your arm straight out to your side. Twirl ball towards your nose and then drop it down in front of your elbow. Now, make a complete circle as you carry the baton so ball is up again. Next,

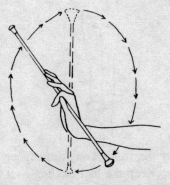
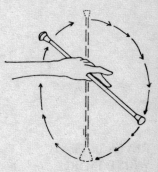

drop the ball down and in toward your shoulder and behind the elbow. Bring it forward and vertical to complete the twirl. Practice this in your left hand, too.

FLAT WRIST TWIRL Keep this twirl as flat as possible. The old name for it was the "pancake." Your arm is straight out at shoulder level, palm down as you hold the baton, Now, twirl the baton toward your body so the ball passes above your arm and the tip passes under it. The baton is always in a horizontal position for this twirl. Practice in both hands.

REVERSE FLAT
WRIST TWIRL

Twirl the baton away from your body. Keep the ball circling over your arm and tip circling under as above. Practice in both hands and remember to keep it flat.

FRONT TWO-HAND Hold your baton in the right hand— thumb to ball. Turn your palm up and catch it between your thumb and first finger. Bring your left hand over, palm up, as if you were asking for money. Now the left hand is above the right hand. Push your left hand to the right with the side of your hand. Catch baton in the left hand.

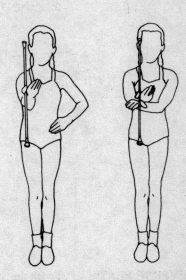

BACK PASS

After your front two-hand, the baton should be in the left hand with your thumb facing down the shaft to the ball. Bring the baton behind your back and keep it close to your body as you pass it to the right hand.

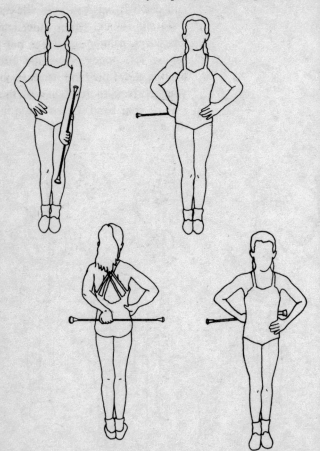

WHIP

Begin holding the baton in the right hand with your thumb to the ball, behind your back. Bring the tip to the front by scooting the baton around an imaginary railroad track—your waist. Now the baton moves vertically, ball up. Then scratch your shoulder with your arm movement. Baton, ball leading, whips out to right side and then comes back behind the back. This is an important twirl. Practice it to perfection.

PALM UP

REVERSE WHIP　　　Continue from the whip, pass to left hand, shoot the tip of the baton out to the left side, bring it up and loop it behind the left arm. Now bring it up straight over your head, then hide it behind your back, as in the whip.

HAND ROLL　　　Begin holding your baton horizontally, palm up. Start turning your hand counterclockwise. Let the baton roll over the top of your wrist.

4-FINGER TWIRL　　　Weave the baton in and out between your fingers and roll across the back of your hand until you

154

are holding it like a pencil—ball up. Always hold your palm up for this twirl. Use the weight of the baton to bring it around.

ELBOW ROLL

Your left hand is in a fist and rests against your throat. Your elbow is lifted and pointed out so that your arm is level. Now, in the right hand, hold your baton, thumb to ball. Your right arm is up and out to the side. Lower your right arm to your side, then bring it under your left arm. Right hand touches the outside of your left arm. With right hand, push baton over your left arm. Baton should roll smoothly to right side, as your right hand moves back to catch it. In this roll, the ball of the baton is pointing up, horizontal, to your right and finally, down to the ground.

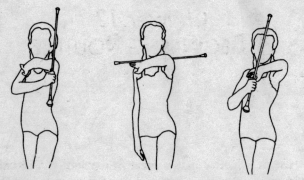

Learning the basics of baton twirling will be easy if you set goals along the way. Annetta Lucero, the world champion twirler, advises young twirlers who are serious about competition to devote three hours a day to "hard but enjoyable" practicing. "But most important of all," Annetta said, "is to keep heading toward your goal.

"If you always have a goal ahead of you, that will keep you going."

Chapter 12
A BEGINNING ROUTINE

Here is a routine that is great for beginners. The only twirl you will need to know is the flat wrist twirl. The basics of drill work are also incorporated.

This routine was choreographed by United States Twirling Association (USTA) coach Janice Ray. Janice made up the routine for her majorette group, the Sunrays. The girls, ages five to thirteen, took first place with this routine at their very first competition. You'll take first place at your school's tryouts, too, if you practice and remember to smile when it's your turn to perform.

Select the song of your choice to accompany your movements for this routine. Make sure the music has a solid, eight count beat. Try counting to eight as you listen to the music and make sure the eight count fits. The ideal twirling music for performance and competition doesn't have any words. Maybe you can use an instrumental version of your favorite popular song.

Sunray Parade March
Choreographed by Janice Ray

Attention position.

Begin marching. Baton tip comes down to ground.
1,2

Bring baton up and extend out from shoulder, straight in front of you.
3,4

Baton comes up and over to salute.
5,6,7,8

With two hands, hold baton horizontal across your thighs and hit them twice.
1,2

Bring baton straight up over head and hit front twice.
3,4

Baton down to thighs, still horizontal. Swing it side to side (r-l-r-l) with head facing right.
5,6,7,8

Repeat hits at thighs and above head and swings for eight.
1,2,3,4,5,6,7,8

Grab baton at center with left hand. Right hand is at your hip. Reverse flat spin with left.
1,2,3,4

Right arm lifts and curves over head with palm flat and facing up to sky. Turn your head to the left and continue twirling.
5,6,7,8

Pass baton to right hand and begin the flat spin.
1,2,3,4

Left arm over head and palm upward, continue flat spin. Head to right.
5,6,7.8

Waist wrap. While turning around to the left in a circle, bring right arm across stomach and pass baton to left side with ball leading. Grab baton with left hand and push horizontal baton across your back. Right arm reaches behind and grabs baton near ball.
1,2,3,4

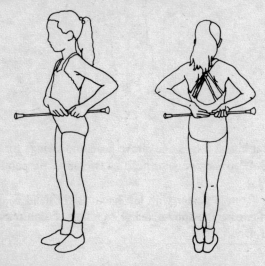

Pull baton to rest on top of right arm and then extend arm straight up and over your head until you are holding baton like a pencil.
5,6,7,8

Lift left arm above your head so two arms are parallel.
1,2,3,4

Both hands come down and rest on hips. Baton remains in right hand.
5,6,7,8

Drop tip off arm and swing baton across to left side with left arm extended out from shoulder. Grab tip with left fingers. Right arm is bent at elbow with ball against left shoulder and covered by fingers. Head follows baton so you are looking down shaft toward left fingers. Step on your left foot and tap with your right foot.
1,2

Step right and tap left as you reverse the movement above.
3,4

Bring baton to chest grabbing with palms facing out. Step and kick your right foot to the left side. Then step and kick your left foot to the right side.
5,6,7,8

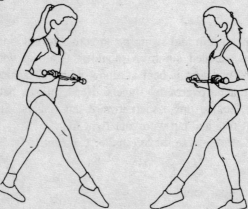

Eight march steps with ball of baton bobbing down at the same time left foot hits the ground. When marching with a group, come together from ranks to form one vertical line.
1,2,3,4,5,6,7,8

Bring right arm and baton up with ball held high as you strut left. Left arm trails behind in a diagonal (two counts). Reverse as you step right and right arm and baton trail low and left hand and arm are up in a diagonal.
1,2,3,4

March for four counts.
5,6,7,8

Repeat strut above to the left and to the right.
1,2,3,4

March for four counts.
5,6,7,8

(In a parade group take another 8 counts to return to ranks.)

Grab baton near tip with palm to front. Bring right knee up and touch ball of baton to side of bended knee (two counts). Step and bring left knee up touching tip to knee. Baton turns over in front of your body, like a steering wheel.
1,2
3,4

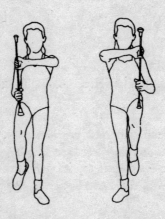

Hold baton horizontal in front of you and push forward. It is straight and still or, as baton twirlers say—a "dead stick."
5,6

Dead stick slaps thighs
7,8

Hold dead stick above head and turn around to left.
1,2,3,4

Return to marching position, holding baton like a pencil.
5,6,7,8

Turn your head right and continue marching with right knee lifting higher than left knee in a hopping movement. Baton remains at rest on top of right arm. Make two full arm circles with right arm—back to front. Left hand on hip.
1,2,3,4

March front for count of four.
5,6,7,8

Repeat hop step and arm circles.
1,2,3,4

March again for four.
5,6,7,8

Slide baton off your arm and across your body to the left side in a horizontal line. Right arm follows baton. Left leg bends in side lunge. Right leg extended. Turn head to left.
1,2

Baton back to resting on arm. Bend right leg in a side lunge and turn head to right. Be sure to hold baton in the center.
3,4

Flat spin and march front.
5,6,7,8

Repeat above sequence . . .

Lunge left.
1,2

Lunge right.
3,4

Flat spin and march.
5,6,7,8

Rest horizontal baton on left shoulder, right elbow points front.
1,2,3,4

Baton points down to ground—tip first.
5,6

Bring baton up to cradle of arm in attention position.
7,8

Step to the left, then step with your right foot, closing your feet together. Step left again. Swing both arms left in a high diagonal. Look left.
1,2

Step right, close, step to the right again with both arms to right in a diagonal. Look right.
3,4

Left hand to waist. Hold baton as an extension of your right arm and circle arm and baton in front of body. Start under and then move it up and over head. Circle once again.
5,6,7,8

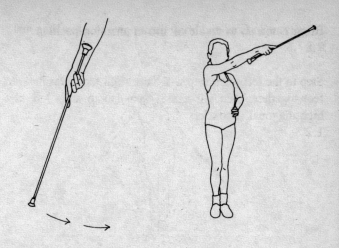

Repeat last eight counts.
1,2,3,4,5,6,7,8

With straight elbows, cross arms in front and bring them up to a high V. The baton remains in right hand.
1,2,3,4

Cross arms in front and bring them down to a low diagonal.
5,6,7,8

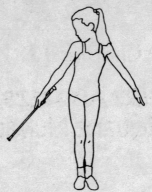

Repeat last eight counts, the bow.
1,2,3,4,5,6,7,8

Resume marching. When in a parade, repeat the entire routine after you hear the whistle command from your lead twirler.

Chapter 13

JERRY ALVAREZ'S
PARADE ROUTINE NUMBER ONE

Twirlers from all over the world travel to the Fresno, California home of Jerry Alvarez to learn custom-choreographed routines from this teacher of champions.

Jerry coached 1982 Senior Women's World Champion Yolanda Castellanos, 1983 winner of the same title Annetta Lucero, and 1984 Men's Champion Mark Nash. "Baton twirling today is more sophisticated than ever before," Jerry said. "The baton is in the air more of the time. Dance and gymnastics are now incorporated. Baton twirling uses more muscles than any other sport."

A specialty in Jerry's routines are the roll sections. Although this movement is considered intermediate, you may want to add a few elbow rolls to your routines after you become more comfortable with the easier tricks. In competitive twirling, the roll section of a routine often lasts for forty-five seconds in a two minute performance. This is a big change from the 1950s, Jerry said.

Back then baton twirlers did about five to ten seconds of rolls.

Jerry Alvarez has taught his original routines to pupils and coaches from around the world. Now, for the benefit of beginning twirlers, he offers Parade Routine Number One for your first competition or majorette tryout.

Parade Routine Number One
Choreographed by Jerry Alvarez

Attention position. Both hands on hips. March for eight counts.
1,2,3,4,5,6,7,8

Rhythm Swing
Uncradle baton so both hands are grasping it from the top. Raise baton higher to left side than right side as you swing arms and baton up, down, up and down.
1,2,3,4

Release baton from left hand and place hand on hip. Brush baton over right leg twice as you look to the right.
5,6,7,8

Repeat two-hand swing as before.
1,2,3,4

Repeat brushes looking right.
5,6,7,8

Take baton behind your back as if you were about to sit on it. Pull it up and all the way underneath your left arm. Turn your head to the left.
1,2,3,4

Take baton across your back the other way and bring it up all the way under the right arm. Head turns to the right.
5,6,7,8

Bring left hand front and grab baton under right elbow. Turn baton over, leading with your left arm. Turn it with

both hands as you would a steering wheel. Baton should be flat and parallel to the floor as it rests on top of right arm and under left arm. Reverse movement and bring baton to rest on top of your left arm.
1,2

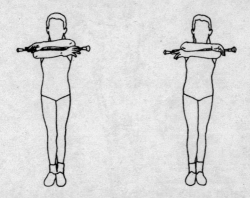

With right arm take baton straight out to your side, elbow straight. Left arm pushes straight out so that arms are in a T. Left palm is up. Head looks to right.
3,4

Bring both arms up above your head. Baton is extended straight up from right hand. Left hand palm is facing in. Head looks up.

5

Bring both arms and baton straight down to the sides of your legs. Head looks down toward toes.

6

Bring baton up to the cradle of your arm and come to attention.
7,8

Military Swing

Mark time as you march with baton. Elbow is bent and wrist moves up and down, tracing half a heart. Poke baton out and up on fourth count.
1,2,3
4

Swing baton back and over in a big circle, looking back to
right. Left hand remains on your hip.
5,6

Come to attention.
7,8

Repeat Military Swing sequence
1,2,3,4,5,6,7,8

Bring baton out of cradle position. Grab it near tip with
your left hand, under your right elbow.
1,2

Taking baton in the left hand, swing it down in front of
your knees and then slap it back into the right hand. Right
hand is palm up.
3,4

Release left hand and take the baton in your right hand.
Turn it over so the center of the shaft is directly beneath

the chin. Now you are grasping the baton with both hands on top. Both elbows rest on each end of baton, creating a straight line.
5,6

Push baton out so hands slide to the ends of the shaft. At the same time, point left toe front and look left.
7

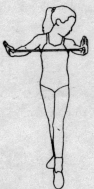

Pull baton back to your chest and under chin as above. Elbows rest on tip and ball creating a straight line, as before.
8

Do four small whips looking straight ahead.
1,2,3,4

Do four large whips as you are facing right.
5,6,7,8

Another whip on right as you look right.
1,2

Pass dead stick behind your back and then do a reverse
whip on your left side. Turn head to the left.
3,4

Pass the baton in back and repeat front whip . . .
5,6

Pass to left and do repeat reverse whip.
7,8

Now, step left and raise your right knee so baton is hitting knee at the center of the shaft.
1,2

Knee comes down. Do a reverse figure eight and pass behind your back as left knee comes up. You are facing right, but turn your head to look at the crowd on the street. 3,4

Still facing right, move down the street sideways with a step-together-step-together march. Left hand is palm up and arm is extended out to left. Do two whips with baton on right side.
5,6,7,8

Repeat the last eight counts, starting again with your right knee up.
1,2,3,4,5,6,7,8

Do a flat figure eight (under, over). Pass above head as you turn 360 degrees to the left and do a two-hand twirl, twice. Baton ends up in left hand. Do a flat figure eight. Release for one loop in air and catch right.
1,2
3,4
5,6
7,8

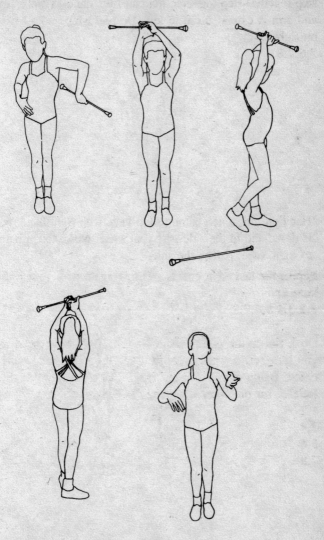

Flat wrist twirl, right hand.
1,2,3,4

Hand on hip, touch baton to left knee with right hand; ball
is down and to the side past your knee. Now, touch baton
to right knee, ball to the side.
5,6

Cradle baton over your right shoulder. You are holding the baton with your hand on top, thumb to ball. Bring your hand up, ball swings behind shoulder and the baton rests behind your arm vertically.

1

Bring baton down to your side, ball points down to ground, and head looks down.

2

Now swing baton up again to cradle over your shoulder as before. Hold the position for a count.

3,4

Swing the baton all the way around in a circle, like a windmill blade. Do a wrist twirl as you move your right arm. Left arm is out and forward, hand outstretched. Look back over right shoulder.
5,6,7,8

Repeat hitch hike sequence starting with count 1, baton coming up, down, up and windmill. End, baton down in your right hand, left hand on hip.
5,6,7,8

Straddle Pass

Look to right as you raise your right knee; the top of your right leg is parallel to the floor. Circle baton and pass under the right leg to your left hand.
1,2

Do a reverse whip with left hand.
3

Now pass baton behind your back to your right hand.
4

Repeat straddle pass, right to left.
5,6,7,8

Shovel Step

Shovel baton to side of right hip, twisting your trunk to the left. Keep looking at the crowd. Repeat for four counts. 1,2,3,4

Pony Trot

Hands are open, facing audience. Baton rests on thumbs. Elbows are bent and in to your sides. Right leg *only* comes up high and turns out at the foot on the trot jump. Move sideways as you trot for four counts. 5,6,7,8

Repeat the shovel and pony trot steps for eight counts.
1,2,3,4,5,6,7,8

Bring baton up vertically alongside your right arm. Left arm is across chest and left hand is near your underarm grasping the ball.
1,2

Right hand slides down baton shaft and down to your side as you bow. Left hand is straight, palm in and flat.
3,4

Attention position and resume marching.
5,6,7,8

(If you wish, add a salute at the beginning and end of the routine.)

Chapter 14
YOU'RE R-E-A-D-Y READY

This is it. Tryout day. Take three deep breaths, then read on to find out what to expect at your cheerleading or baton twirling tryout.

It's natural to be nervous at a tryout or competition. Each girl has her own way of expressing feelings of excitement, anticipation and anxiety during a tryout. Don't let your reactions be a surprise on tryout day. A good way to find out how you will react is to hold practice tryouts at home.

At a practice tryout, do your routine all the way through with friends or relatives watching. Ask them not to laugh or stop you if you make a mistake. Before you begin, take a few moments to imagine the scene in your school gym on tryout day. Imagine yourself standing outside the door of the gym with a number pinned on your hip. Looking at all the other girls waiting, do you imagine that their routines are better than your own? Practice putting aside negative thoughts like these and think instead of your own routine.

As you walk into the gym—actually the living room—at

your practice tryout, check your feelings. Is there a particular moment when you are unusually nervous or tense? If so, practice the movement you are doing at that moment until it becomes natural. The trick to practice tryouts is to visualize yourself in the real situation. That way you have a chance to notice and overcome nervous habits or actions that may detract from your performance.

Annetta Lucero, the world champion twirler, burst into tears before her performance in Italy. She then went on to win the world title. From her practices, Annetta knew that a few tears wouldn't hurt her performance. She was in tune with her own signs of nervousness and knew how to keep them under control.

One secret many cheerleaders and baton twirlers have learned is that the real competition is not with the other girls. At each performance or tryout, these girls know they are competing with themselves to do their very best. There won't be any disappointments at your tryout if you focus on your own performance, instead of speculating about the chances other girls will have to win.

Try not to talk away your nervousness on the day of the tryout. You certainly won't hurt the other girls' feelings if you are quiet. The energy you might spend bragging about your routine or talking about who has a good chance to make the squad would be better spent thinking silently about your own performance. You've heard the old saying "Silence is golden." Try using some silence before your tryout to help you attain your golden wish—a spot on the cheerleading squad or twirling team.

There are some common characteristics judges will look for at both baton and cheerleading tryouts. Make sure you've prepared a winning look in these judging categories:

1. Appearance—Neat and conventional. Hair is off your face.
2. Movements—Good flexibility and flow.
3. Skills—Basic baton or cheerleading moves are mastered. Good technique in all twirls and cheerleading positions.
4. Originality—Performance shows your unique capabilities and imagination.
5. Spirit—Your performance gets across the message that you absolutely *love* cheerleading or baton twirling.

Here's another winning secret: Don't get bogged down in last minute preparations. Be sure you arrive at the gym at least fifteen minutes before your competition or tryout.

Before a big race, runners prepare by eating lightly. Keep your proper eating habits in mind during the days before your tryout. Eating a big meal at lunch the day before your tryout will not reduce your nervousness. It will make you sluggish and take your energy away. You'll want to be light on your feet on tryout day, so remember to eat light.

There will be a handful of judges at your cheerleading tryout. Typically a judging panel will include spirit advisors from neighboring schools, a college cheerleader, a local dance teacher, your school's vice principal and the spirit advisor from your own school. These adult judges will use a scoring sheet to rate your performance. Study the example of a typical score sheet from a high school tryout (Table 1).

Did you notice that beauty and popularity are not included on the tryout score sheet? Cheerleaders today are selected for their very specialized athletic ability and their willingness to be a good representative of their school.

At some schools, spirit advisors conduct a personal interview in addition to the tryout. Prepare for this by studying the requirements for cheerleaders set down in your student government constitution. Once you know the requirements, you will be able to think about them at home and write down the ways that you fulfill each one. Here is an example of the requirements for cheerleader conduct from a high school student constitution:

Section IX—Conduct

A. General Conduct
1. Be a lady at all times.
2. Be neat and well-groomed always.
3. Observe all rules of the school regarding conduct.
4. Be friendly to everyone.
5. Use proper language at all times.
6. No smoking and no drinking. Intoxication of any kind during school hours or at any school event is grounds for immediate dismissal from the squad.
7. Be willing to sacrifice personal desires to benefit the squad.
8. Be willing to take criticism.
9. Always put the school above personal interests.
10. A high moral standard must be maintained.

Keeping in mind the requirements your school has set for cheerleaders, take a piece of paper and write your answers to the following questions from a typical cheerleader interview.

1. Why do you want to be a cheerleader?
2. Can you give in when the majority votes against your feelings? Explain:

3. Are you easily offended? Are you a patient person? Are you stubborn?
4. How would you go about keeping spirit up at the end of the year?
5. How do you feel about cheering for girls' sports?
6. What ideas do you have for pep rallies?
7. Will you be able to make being a cheerleader your highest priority over a job, boyfriend or other sports?

The last question asked is perhaps the most important in your tryout interview. You have already made a commitment to preparing for your new role as a spirit leader through exercise, diet, practice and other preparations. Give some thought now to the extra dedication it will take to keep up practice and performance commitments once you make the cheerleading squad or baton twirling team. Look at the page from a spirit advisor's calendar to see the incredible amount of activity cheerleaders are required to keep up with, once they make the team (Table 2).

Tryouts for a baton twirling team have many of the same characteristics as cheerleading tryouts. Perhaps the biggest difference is that piece of metal which can go sprawling across the floor of the gym at any moment. When that happens, there is only one way to handle the situation. Quickly run and pick up the baton. Then, pick up the routine at the point you left off, or, if there is music, the point that goes with the song. When twirlers perform at competitions, parades or tryouts without dropping their baton it is a rarity. A ''no-drop'' routine is the ideal and does win points from the judges. One sure way to lose points, though, is to lose your smile and poise. It's no fun to watch a performance when the twirler loses her smile every time she makes a mistake.

Once you are part of a marching baton twirling group, the suspense of tryouts and competition continues at each parade. Judges sit above the street on a reviewing stand, usually located near the end of the parade route. They score each twirling group on marching, showmanship and twirling skills. Take a look at a scoring sheet from a parade to see what judges expect to find in a winning group (Table 3).

Opportunities to compete in solo twirling competitions are multiplying almost as quickly as the number of beginning baton twirlers. Two baton organizations sponsor state, regional and national competitions. They are the United States Twirling Association and the National Baton Twirling Association. Competition requirements are different for these associations, so be sure to know what the judging criteria are before you enter.

When some people take a long journey, they have the attitude that getting to their destination is part of the fun. When you started reading this book, you had only a small chance of becoming a spirit leader. As you continued reading, you made a commitment to practice and preparation. The moment you decided, ''I will,'' you were half way to your goal.

With your positive attitude, learning the basics of cheerleading and baton twirling was fun. Putting the basics to work in the routines you learned was even more fun. Maybe you agonized over your first practice tryout at home or the after-school workshops; but you made new friends along the way and found out you weren't afraid to try. Reading back in your special baton or cheerleading notebook, you will realize how far you've come since you saw your chance to become someone special.

Now it's tryout day. One-by-one sixty girls have gone

behind the locked doors to perform their routines. Finally, the spirit advisor walks out of the locked gym and puts up a list of names. As you crowd around the bulletin board with the other girls, you take some deep breaths. Then—a rush of excitement hits you like a bolt.

There is your name at the top of the list. Congratulations! You made it.

Table 1
Judging score sheet for a cheerleader tryout.

```
                    PIONEER VARSITY PEPSTER TRYOUTS

CIRCLE ONE                                      CIRCLE ONE

   ORIGINAL ROUTINE                                YELL
   GROUP ROUTINE                                   FLAG
                                                   SONG
GIRLS NUMBER_____
```

CATEGORY	CHECK( ) NEEDS IMPROVEMENT		CIRCLE (0) VERY GOOD
ORIGINALITY	DIFFICULTY VARIETY REPETITION NOVELTY TRICKS(FLAG ONLY)		SUPERIOR EXCELLENT GOOD FAIR NEEDS WORK SCORE---------(0-25)
EXECUTION	PRECISION FOOTWORK LEG MOVES VOICE JUMPS	ARMS FINGERS HANDS KICKS SPLITS	SUPERIOR EXCELLENT GOOD FAIR NEEDS WORK SCORE---------(0-25)
COORDINATION	RHYTHM TIMING CONTINUITY POISE		SUPERIOR EXCELLENT GOOD FAIR NEEDS WORK SCORE---------(0-25)
SHOWMANSHIP	PEP SMILE CONFIDENCE PERSONALITY PROJECTION EYE CONTACT SPIRIT SNAP AND FLASH		SUPERIOR EXCELLENT GOOD FAIR NEEDS WORK SCORE-------(0-25)
APPEARANCE	UNIFORM NEATNESS		SUPERIOR EXCELLENT GOOD FAIR SCORE---------(0-10)
JUDGES SIGNATURE			TOTAL---------(110)

Table 2
Monday through Friday calendar of a busy spirit advisor.

MONDAY	TUESDAY	WEDNESDAY	THURSDAY	FRIDAY
2/14 ♡'s DAY — MAGIC MOUNTAIN CONTEST PRACTICE 3:00-5:00 — LAST WEEK OF WINTER SPORTS →	**2/15** BOYS V/JV SOCCER vs. BELL GARDEN 3:00-4:30 — ALL SQUADS — BATON PRACTICE NORTH FIELD	**2/16** GIRLS V/JV SOCCER at CAL HI — BATON & JV TEAMS — MAGIC MTN. CONTEST PRACTICE 3:00-5:00	**2/17** BOYS Varsity Soccer at WHITTIER — ALL SQUADS	**2/18** MAGIC MT. PRACTICE 3:00-5:30
2/21 1ST WEEK OF SPRING SPORTS SEASON → GO TITANS Keep up the Spirit!	**2/15 [2/22]** VARSITY CHEER MAGIC MTN. PRACTICE — JVs-PAINT SIGNS for TRACK — BATON PRACTICE WITH BAND N.F.	**2/23** KEVIN SOLO ROUTINES Berry, M.J., Julie — FROSH CHEER/ BAKE COOKIES — MAGIC MTN. PRACTICE 3:00-5:00	**2/24** BOYS & GIRLS TRACK vs. ROSEMEAD Here 3:00-4:30 ALL SQUADS — Signs up at lunch? — MAGIC MT. PRACTICE 4:30-6:00	**2/25** PLAN: SUPER-PEP RALLY for all Spring Sports — LAST PRACTICE for MAGIC MTN COMPETITION /\
SUNDAY 2/27 Bus leaves 8:30 a.m. — MAGIC MT. REGIONAL CHEER-LEADING CHAMPIONSHIP 1st step: — FINALS OF COMPETITION MAR. 6S	**3/1** BOYS V/JV SOFTBALL vs. ARROYO Here-5:00 — B&G V/JV SWIMMING vs. TEMPLE CITY 3:00-HERE	**3/2** VAR. BASEBALL vs. EL MONTE 3:15 HERE — BATON TWIRLERS + BAND PRACTICE - NORTH FIELD	SPRING SPORTS SEASON INCLUDES: ① TRACK ② SWIMMING ③ TENNIS ④ GOLF ⑤ BASEBALL ⑥ SOFTBALL ⑦ BOYS VOLLEYBALL — IMPORTANT DATES: ① STATE - 3/2, ② SUPER-PEP rally 3/3, ③ VAR. ROSTER TRYOUT MISSING 3/5, ④ VAR. PEPSTER WORKSHOPS - 2 wks. 3/15 - 3/26	⑤ TRYOUTS Saturday 3/12 9:00-5:00 Boys Baseball, ⑥ TWIRLES Review 4/23, ⑦ PROM 4/30

Table 3
A scoring sheet used by judges at a parade.

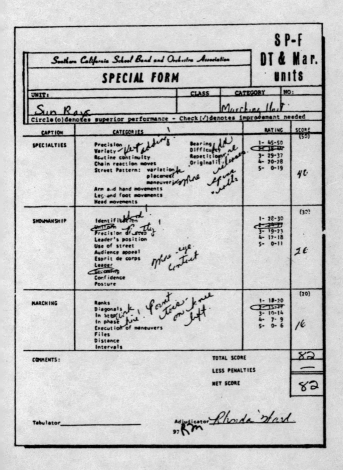

Southern California School Band and Orchestra Association

SP-F DT & Mar. units

SPECIAL FORM

UNIT: Sun Rays	CLASS	CATEGORY: Marching Unit	NO:

Circle (o) denotes superior performance – Check (✓) denotes improvement needed

CAPTION	CATEGORIES		RATING	SCORE
SPECIALTIES	Precision Bearing		1- 45-50	(50)
	Variety Difficulty		2- 38-44	
	Routine continuity Repetition		3- 29-37	
	Chain reaction moves Originality		4- 20-28	
	Street Pattern: variation placement maneuvering		5- 0-19	40
	Arm and hand movements			
	Leg and foot movements			
	Head movements			
SHOWMANSHIP	Identification		1- 28-30	(30)
	Uniform		2- 24-27	
	Precision of moves		3- 19-23	
	Leader's position		4- 17-18	
	Use of street		5- 0-11	
	Audience appeal			
	Esprit de corps			26
	Leader			
	Decorum			
	Confidence			
	Posture			
MARCHING	Ranks		1- 18-20	(20)
	Diagonals		2- 15-17	
	In step		3- 10-14	
	In phase		4- 7- 9	
	Execution of maneuvers		5- 0- 6	16
	Files			
	Distance			
	Intervals			

COMMENTS:	TOTAL SCORE	82
	LESS PENALTIES	—
	NET SCORE	82

Tabulator _____

Adjudicator _Rhoda Hard_

About the Author

Susan Rogerson Smith is a native Southern Californian. She was born and raised within the sound of the campanile bells on the UCLA campus in Westwood Village. On any Big-Game Day, the early-morning sound of UCLA's Marching Band was her alarm clock, and spirit sports became an early fascination.

Miss Smith attended (all-girl) Marlborough School; while there she tried out for, and was selected as, the first ''girl'' cheerleader in the 89-year history of Los Angeles's oldest, all-male college prepartory school, Loyola High.

Miss Smith earned her Bachelor's degree in Journalism from the University of California, Berkeley, and has since pursued an active career in corporate communications and free-lance writing.